Essential Russian

Written by
Constantine Muravnik

LIVING LANGUAGE®

Published in the United States by Living Language, an imprint of Random House, Inc.

www.livinglanguage.com

Editor: Erin Quirk
Production Editor: Ciara Robinson
Production Manager: Tom Marshall
Audio Producer: Ok Hee Kolwitz
Interior Design: Sophie Chin
Illustrations: Sophie Chin

First Edition

ISBN: 978-0-307-97209-5

This book is available at special discounts for bulk purchases for sales promotions or premiums. Special editions, including personalized covers, excerpts of existing books, and corporate imprints, can be created in large quantities for special needs. For more information, write to Special Markets/ Premium Sales, 1745 Broadway, MD 3-1, New York, New York 10019 or e-mail specialmarkets@ randomhouse.com.

PRINTED IN THE UNITED STATES OF AMERICA

10 9 8 7 6 5 4 3

About the Author

Constantine Muravnik is a native of Moscow. He holds a Ph.D. from the Slavic Department of Yale University, where he has been teaching since 1995. Prior to this, he taught Russian in the Slavic Department of Georgetown University and at Moscow State University, where he earned his B.A.

Acknowledgments

Thanks to the Living Language team: Amanda D'Acierno, Christopher Warnasch, Suzanne McQuade, Laura Riggio, Heather Dalton, Fabrizio LaRocca, Siobhan O'Hare, Sophie Chin, Ann McBride, Tina Malaney, Sue Daulton, Alison Skrabek, Ciara Robinson, and Tom Marshall.

Course Outline

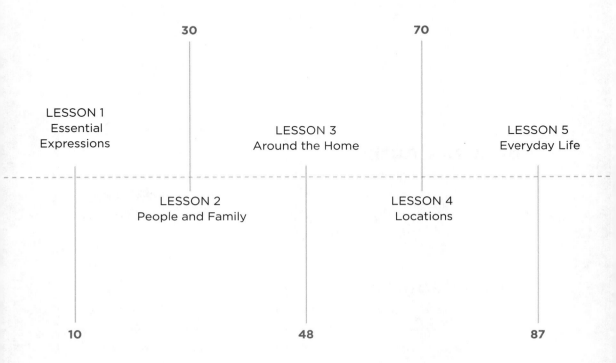

30

70

LESSON 1
Essential
Expressions

LESSON 3
Around the Home

LESSON 5
Everyday Life

LESSON 2
People and Family

LESSON 4
Locations

10

48

87

COURSE

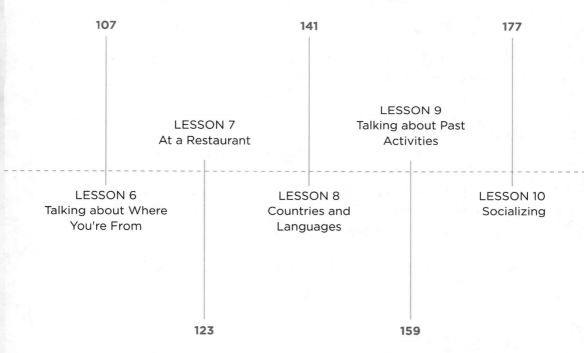
OUTLINE

How To Use This Course

здра́вствуйте!

Welcome to *Living Language Essential Russian*! Ready to learn how to speak, read, and write Russian?

Before we begin, let's go over what you'll see in this course. It's very easy to use, but this section will help you get started.

PHONETICS

The first five lessons of this course contain phonetics (in other words, [spah-SEE-bə] in addition to спаси́бо) to help you get started with Russian pronunciation. However, please keep in mind that phonetics are not exact—they are just a general approximation of sounds—and thus you should rely most on the audio, *not* the phonetics, to improve your pronunciation skills.

For a guide to our phonetics system, see the Pronunciation Guide at the end of the course.

LESSONS

There are 10 lessons in this course. Each lesson is divided into three parts and has the following components:

Welcome at the beginning outlining what you will cover in each of the three parts of the lesson.

PART 1

- **Vocabulary Builder 1** listing the key words and phrases for that lesson.
- **Vocabulary Practice 1** to practice what you learned in Vocabulary Builder 1.

- **Grammar Builder 1** to guide you through the structure of the Russian language (how to form sentences, questions, and so on).

PART 2

- **Vocabulary Builder 2** listing more key words and phrases.

- **Vocabulary Practice 2** to practice what you learned in Vocabulary Builder 2.

- **Grammar Builder 2** for more information on language structure.

- **Work Out 1** for a comprehensive practice of what you've learned so far.

PART 3

- **Bring It All Together** to put what you've learned in a conversational context through a dialogue, monologue, description, or other similar text.

- **Work Out 2** for another helpful practice exercise.

- **Drive It Home** to ingrain an important point of Russian structure for the long term.

- **Parting Words** outlining what you learned in the lesson.

Take It Further

Take It Further sections are scattered throughout the lesson to provide extra information about the new vocabulary you just saw, expand on some grammar points, or introduce additional words and phrases.

WORD RECALL

Word Recall sections appear in between lessons. They review important vocabulary and grammar from previous lessons, including the one you just finished. These sections will reinforce what you've learned so far in the course, and help you retain the information for the long term.

QUIZZES

This course contains two quizzes: **Quiz 1** is halfway through the course (after Lesson 5), and **Quiz 2** appears after the last lesson (Lesson 10). The quizzes are self-graded so it's easy for you to test your progress and see if you should go back and review.

REVIEW DIALOGUES

There are five **Review Dialogues** at the end of the course, after Quiz 2. These everyday dialogues review what you learned in Lessons 1-10, introduce some new vocabulary and structures, and allow you to become more familiar with conversational Russian. Each dialogue is followed by comprehension questions that serve as the course's final review.

PROGRESS BAR

You will see a **Progress Bar** on almost every page that has course material. It indicates your current position in the course and lets you know how much progress you're making. Each line in the bar represents a lesson, with the final line representing the Review Dialogues.

AUDIO

Look for this symbol ⊙ to help guide you through the audio as you're reading the book. It will tell you which track to listen to for each section that has audio. When you see the symbol, select the indicated track and start listening! If you don't see the symbol, then there isn't any audio for that section.

The audio can be used on its own—in other words, without the book—when you're on the go. Whether in your car or at the gym, you can listen to the audio to brush up on your pronunciation, review what you've learned in the book, or even use it as a standalone course.

PRONUNCIATION GUIDE, GRAMMAR SUMMARY, AND WRITING GUIDE

At the back of this book you will find a **Pronunciation Guide**, **Grammar Summary**, and **Writing Guide**. The Pronunciation Guide provides information on the Cyrillic alphabet and the phonetics system used to teach Russian pronunciation in this course. The Grammar Summary contains a helpful, brief overview of key points in the Russian grammar system. The Writing Guide provides examples and tips for handwriting the Cyrillic alphabet as well as some practice activities.

FREE ONLINE TOOLS

Go to **www.livinglanguage.com/languagelab** to access your free online tools. The tools are organized around the lessons in this course, with audiovisual flashcards, interactive games and quizzes, and additional audio practice for each lesson. These tools will help you review and practice the vocabulary and grammar that you've seen in the lessons, as well as provide some extra words and phrases related to the lesson's topic. The additional audio practice can be downloaded for use on the go.

Lesson 1: Essential Expressions

Пе́рвый уро́к: Основны́е выраже́ния

[PER-vyhi oo-ROK: ahs-nahv-NY-i vy-rah-ZHE-nee-yuh]

Добро́ пожа́ловать! [dah-BRAW pah-ZHAH-lə-vət'] *Welcome!* In this first lesson, you'll learn some basic expressions and other useful words, phrases, and grammar points to get you started speaking Russian. You'll learn how to:

☐ Greet someone and ask how they're doing.

☐ Use basic courtesy expressions.

☐ Ask simple questions when you meet someone.

☐ Use both formal and informal forms of address.

☐ Recognize masculine and feminine nouns.

☐ Put it all together in a simple conversation between two people meeting for the first time.

But let's begin with some essential vocabulary. Ready?
Remember to look for this symbol ▶ to help guide you through the audio as you're reading the book. It will tell you which track to listen to for each section that has audio. When you see the symbol, select the indicated track and start listening. If you don't see the symbol, then there isn't any audio for that section.

Vocabulary Builder 1

▶ 1A Vocabulary Builder 1 (CD: 1, Track 2)

Hello! (pl. or sg. form.)	здра́вствуйте	ZDRAH-stvəi-ti
Hello! (sg. inform.)	здра́вствуй	ZDRAH-stvəi
Hi! or Hey there! (inform.)	приве́т	pri-VʲET
Mr.	господи́н	gəs-pah-DEEN
Mrs. or Ms.	госпожа́	gəs-pah-ZHAH
Nice to meet you! (lit., Very pleasant!)	О́чень прия́тно!	AW-chin' pri-YAT-nə
businessperson (male or female)	бизнесме́н	beez-nes-MEN
businesswoman (less common)	бизнесву́мен, бизнесме́нка *(coll.)*	beez-nes-VU-men, beez-nes-MEN-kə
journalist (male)	журнали́ст	zhur-nah-LEEST
journalist (female)	журнали́стка	zhur-nah-LEEST-kə
American (male)	америка́нец	ah-mi-ri-KAH-nits
American (female)	америка́нка	ah-mi-ri-KAHN-kə
Welcome! (to a visitor)	Добро́ пожа́ловать!	dah-BRAW pah-ZHAH-lə-vət'
Good-bye.	До свида́ния.	də-svi-DAH-ni-yə
Thank you.	Спаси́бо.	spah-SEE-bə

You'll see phonetics in the first five lessons of *Essential Russian* to help you get started reading. For a guide to the phonetic system used here, see the Pronunciation Guide at the end of the course. Take note that stress marks [´] used in all textbooks of Russian, including this one, are meant to help you learn and memorize the rhythmic structure of Russian words; however, they are never printed in authentic Russian materials, and you won't see them over the letter

Ë/ë, which is always stressed. Pay attention to the way Russian vowels sound in stressed and unstressed syllables. And finally, be aware that prepositions blend with the following words and thus are pronounced as one phonetic word with one stress, e.g., до свидáния [də-svi-DAH-ni-yə].

You'll also need to learn how to write the Cyrillic alphabet. For a guide on handwritten Cyrillic, refer to the Writing Guide in the appendix. There you'll find examples of handwritten Cyrillic and activities to give you a chance to practice your handwriting.

✎ Vocabulary Practice 1

Now let's practice what you've learned! Fill in the blanks with the correct Russian translations of the following phrases. If you don't remember some of them, that's fine. You can always go back over the vocabulary builder section and review.

1. *Mr.* ГОСПОДИН

2. *Thank you.* СПОСИБО

3. *businessman* БИЗНесМАН

4. *Good-bye.* До СВеДАНЯ

5. *American (male)* АМЕРИКАНеЦ

6. *Nice to meet you!* ОЧЕН ПВИАТНА

7. *journalist (male)* ЖУВНАЛИЦ

8. *Mrs. or Ms.* ГОСПОЖА

9. *Hello (sg. inform.)* ПРИВеТ

10. *Welcome!* ДобРО ПОЖАЛИВеТ

11. *journalist (female)*   ЖУРНАЛСТКА

12. *Hello (pl./sg. form.)*   ЗДРАСВОТЕ

13. *Hey there! (inform.)*   ЗДРАСВОУЙ

14. *American (female)*   АМЕРИКАНСКА

15. *businesswoman*   БИЗНЕСВУМЕН

ANSWER KEY 1. господи́н; 2. спаси́бо; 3. бизнесме́н; 4. до свида́ния; 5. америка́нец; 6. О́чень прия́тно! 7. журнали́ст; 8. госпожа́; 9. здра́вствуй; 10. Добро́ пожа́ловать! 11. журнали́стка; 12. здра́вствуйте; 13. приве́т; 14. америка́нка; 15. бизнесме́н/бизнесву́ман/бизнесме́нка

Grammar Builder 1

▶ 1B Grammar Builder 1 (CD: 1, Track: 3)

RUSSIAN SINGULAR PRONOUNS AND GENDER

The Russian greeting здра́вствуйте (*hello*) is a command that literally means *be healthy*. Notice that there are two ways of saying *hello*. One is formal; you'd use it with strangers and in formal situations; it has the plural/formal imperative ending, –те. The other, здра́вствуй, is informal; it is used in the singular (i.e., addressing one person) with family members, close friends, peers, and children. This distinction between formal and informal is also made in Russian in the pronouns for the word *you*. Let's take a look at all of the subject pronouns in Russian, starting with the ones referring to just one person.

я	*I*
ты (*inform.*)	*you*
он	*he or it (if masculine, i.e., ending in a consonant)*
она́	*she or it (if feminine, i.e., ending in a vowel or sometimes the soft sign)*
оно́	*it (if neuter, i.e., ending in -o or -e)*

вы (*form.*)	*you (singular)*

As you can see, there are two forms of the singular *you* in the table above. Ты is informal; вы is formal.

Notice that the third person singular pronoun is either masculine (он) or feminine (она́). It can also be neuter (оно́) when it replaces a neuter inanimate noun, such as вино́ (*wine*). We call these distinctions "gender." All Russian singular nouns, whether they refer to human beings or inanimate things, have gender.

You can see that the nouns бизнесме́н (*businessman*) and рестора́н (*restaurant*) are masculine because both end in a consonant, just like the masculine personal pronoun он. On the other hand, the nouns америка́нка (*female American*) and маши́на (*car*) are feminine because they end in an a, just like the feminine personal pronoun она́. It is important to know that the Russian pronouns он, она́, and the plural form, они́ (*they*) can refer to human beings as well as to inanimate objects while оно́ refers only to inanimate objects. Only third person Russian pronouns have gender; all others are "gender blind." Russian pronouns are rarely omitted from the sentence even though they may seem redundant, as the verb ending clearly indicates the referent.

Take It Further 1
▶ 1C Take It Further (CD: 1, Track: 4)

All vowels in Russian words, except for the stressed vowel, are reduced and otherwise altered. When you read and memorize Russian words and expressions, be aware of the way the vowels behave.

Let's take a look at some examples to see how this reduction rule works. When an unstressed a or o appears in the syllable just before the stressed vowel or at the beginning of the word, they are reduced to a kind of short [ah]; in all other positions, the unstressed a and o are pronounced as [ə]. For example, the word молоко́ (*milk*) has three o's but all three are pronounced differently: the first o precedes the stress by more than one syllable, so it is pronounced as a [ə]; the second o is located right before the stressed syllable, therefore it is pronounced as a shorter a [ah]; and only the final o is pronounced fully because it is stressed –[mə-lah-KOH]. Compare the way the underlined vowels sound in the following words:

господи́н [gəs-pah-DEEN]
спаси́бо [spah-SEE-bə]
америка́нка [ah-mi-ri-KAHN-kə]
до свида́ния [dəs-vi-DAH-ni-yə]
добро́ пожа́ловать [dah-BRAW pah-ZHAH-lə-vət']
госпожа́ [gəs-pah-ZHAH]

The unstressed е and я are also reduced to a shorter version of an и [i] (apart from when they appear in some grammatical endings, where they would be pronounced as a [ə]). For example, in the word телефо́н (*telephone*) the first and second e are pronounced as [i], although the first e/[i] is slightly shorter because it precedes the stress by more than one syllable—[ti-li-FAWN]. Compare the way the underlined vowels sound in the following words:

до свида́ния [də-svi-DAH-ni-yə]
здра́вствуйте [ZDRAH-stvəi-ti]
америка́нец [ah-mi-ri-KAH-nits]
о́чень прия́тно [AW-chin' pri-YAT-nə]
приве́т [pri-VʲET]

Vocabulary Builder 2

▶ 1D Vocabulary Builder 2 (CD: 1, Track: 5)

How are you?	Как дела́?	kahk dee-LAH
Well. (I'm well.)	Хорошо́.	hə-rah-SHOH
Do you speak Russian?	Вы говори́те по-ру́сски?	vy gə-vah-REE-ti pah-ROOS-ki
Yes.	Да.	dah
No.	Нет.	nʲet
A little bit.	Немно́го.	nim-NO-gə
gentlemen or ladies and gentlemen	господа́	gəs-pah-DAH
I am an American. (male)	Я америка́нец.	yah ah-mi-ri-KAH-nits
I am an American. (female)	Я америка́нка.	yah ah-mi-ri-KAH-nkə
I am a student. (male)	Я студе́нт.	yah stoo-DʲENT
I am a student. (female)	Я студе́нтка.	yah stoo-DʲENT-kə
Excuse me. (sg. inform.)	Извини́.	iz-vi-NI
Excuse me. (pl./sg. form.)	Извини́те.	iz-vi-NI-ti
Let's go! (sg. inform.)	Пойдём!	pahi-DʲOM
Let's go! (pl./sg. form.)	Пойдёмте!	pahi-DʲOM-ti
Please! or You're welcome!	Пожа́луйста!	pah-ZHAH-lə-stə

Take It Further 2

Notice that the sentence *I'm an American* has only two words in Russian. This is because Russian doesn't have articles (*a, an,* or *the*) and doesn't normally use the verb *to be* in the present tense. So the sentence Я америка́нец is grammatically correct although it literally translates as *I American*; Я Джон is equivalent to the English *I'm John*.

✎ Vocabulary Practice 2

How would you translate the following sentences into Russian?

1. *I'm an American. (male)*   Я американец

2. *I'm a student. (female)*   Я студенка

3. *He's a student.*   Он студент

4. *Let's go! (when speaking to Sasha and Igor)*   Пойдём

5. *She's an American.*   Она американка

6. *Excuse me. (at a business meeting)*   Извините Извините

7. *Do you speak Russian? Yes, a little bit.*   Вы говорите по-русски? Да, немного.

8. *How are you? [I'm] well.*   Как дела? хорошо Спасиба Спасиба

ANSWER KEY
1. Я америка́нец. 2. Я студе́нтка. 3. Он студе́нт. 4. Пойдёмте. 5. Она́ америка́нка. 6. Извини́те.
7. Вы говори́те по-ру́сски? Да, немно́го. 8. Как дела́? Хорошо́.

Grammar Builder 2
▶ 1E Grammar Builder 2 (CD: 1, Track: 6)

RUSSIAN PLURAL PRONOUNS

Now let's look at the personal pronouns that refer to more than one person.

мы	we
вы (pl.)	you
они́	they

Russian plural forms don't have gender. Мы, вы, and они́ refer equally to males and females. Notice that the pronoun вы can be either singular or plural. When it is singular, it refers to one person in the formal sense. When it is plural, there is no distinction between formal and informal.

⊕ Culture Note

The Russian question, Как дела́? (*How are you?*), has more literal significance than its English equivalent: the Russian question actually asks about one's well-being, which presumes that you know the person you're addressing. Accordingly, it would be odd to enter a store and greet an unfamiliar salesperson with this phrase. On the other hand, it is perfectly acceptable among friends and acquaintances.

It is also uncommon to greet the same person with здра́вствуйте, приве́т, or Как дела́? more than once a day. If on a given day you happen to run into the same person several times, you simply acknowledge the encounter with a nod, a smile, etc., or preface your consequent greeting with the phrase ещё раз [i-SHCHOH-rahs] (*once again*). Otherwise, if you greet a person the second time without any reference to your prior meeting the same day, that person might think that you've already forgotten about it.

✎ Work Out 1

▶ 1F Work Out 1 (CD: 1, Track: 7)

Now let's review some of the expressions that you've learned in this lesson. Listen to the Russian audio, and fill in the missing words. Repeat the correct answers in the pauses provided for practice.

1. *Hello! How are you? (form.)*

   Здра́вствуйте! Как ___дела___ ?

2. *Are you an American? (male)*

   Вы ___америка́нец___?

3. *I'm John.*

   Я Джон.

   Nice to meet you.

   ___Очень Приятно___ ! Приято

4. *Thank you and good-bye!*

   Спаси́бо и до ___Свидания___ ! Свидания

5. *Welcome!*

   close!

   Добро́ ___Пожаловать___ ! Пожаловать

6. *Are you a student? (female)*

   Вы студе́нтка?

   Yes, I am a student.

   Да, ___Я студентка___

7. *Do you speak Russian?*

Вы ___Таворими___ по-ру́сски? *Говорите*

8. *Are you a journalist? (male)*

Вы журнали́ст?

No, I am a businessman.

___Нет, я___ бизнесме́н.

ANSWER KEY
1. дела; 2. америка́нец; 3. Очень прия́тно; 4. свида́ния; 5. пожа́ловать; 6. студе́нтка; 7. говори́те; 8. Нет, я

🔊 Bring It All Together
▶ 1G Bring It All Together (CD: 1, Track: 8)

Now let's bring it all together, adding a little more vocabulary and structure. Imagine a dialogue between Irina Smirnova from Russia who is meeting John Smith from the United States. As earlier, you'll hear each phrase in English first and then in Russian.

Irina:	*Hello! Are you Mr. Smith?*
Ирина:	Здра́вствуйте! Вы господи́н Смит?
	[ZDRAH-stvəi-ti vy gəs-pah-DEEN SMIT]
John:	*Yes, I am John Smith.*
Джон:	Да, я Джон Смит.
	[DAH YA DZHAWN SMIT]
Irina:	*Are you an American?*
Ирина:	Вы америка́нец?
	[vy ah-mi-ri-KAH-nits]
John:	*Yes, I am an American. I am a businessman.*
Джон:	Да, я америка́нец. Я бизнесме́н.
	[DAH ya ah-mi-ri-KAH-nits yah beez-nes-MEN]
Irina:	*Nice to meet you! And I am Irina Smirnova. I am Russian.*

Ирина:	Óчень прия́тно! А я Ири́на Смирно́ва. Я ру́сская.
	[AW-chin' pri-IAHT-nə ah-YAH i-REE-nə smir-NAW-və ya ROOS-kə-iah]
John:	*Nice to meet you!*
Джон:	Óчень прия́тно!
	[AW-chin' pri-IAHT-nə]
Irina:	*Do you speak Russian?*
Ирина:	Вы говори́те по-ру́сски?
	[vy gə-vah-REE-ti pah-ROOS-ki]
John:	*Yes, a little bit.*
Джон:	Да, немно́го.
	[DAH nim-NAW-gə]
Irina:	*You speak Russian well.*
Ирина:	Вы хорошо́ говори́те по-ру́сски!
	[vy hə-rah-SHOH gə-vah-REE-ti pah-ROOS-ki]
John:	*Thank you. Are you a journalist?*
Джон:	Спаси́бо. А вы журнали́стка?
	[spah-SEE-bə ah-VY zhur-nah-LEEST-kə]
Irina:	*Yes, I am a journalist.*
Ирина:	Да, я журнали́стка.
	[DAH ya zhur-nah-LEEST-kə]
John:	*[I am] very glad (to meet you), Ms. Smirnova.*
Джон:	Óчень рад, госпожа́ Смирно́ва.
	[AW-chin' RAHD gəs-pah-ZHAH smir-NAW-və]
Irina:	*You can just call me Irina. (lit., It's OK just Irina.)*
Ирина:	Мо́жно про́сто Ири́на.
	[MAWZH-nə PROS-tə i-REE-nə]
John:	*Good. Thank you, Irina.*
Джон:	Хорошо́. Спаси́бо, Ири́на.
	[hə-rah-SHOH spah-SEE-bə i-REE-nə]
Irina:	*Well, John, let's go. (Shall we go?)*
Ирина:	Ну что, Джон, пойдёмте?
	[noo-SHTAW DZHAWN pahi-DʲOM-ti]

Lesson 1: Essential Expressions   **21**

John:	*Let's go, Irina.*
Джон:	Пойдёмте, Ири́на!
	[pahi-DʲOM-ti i-REE-nə]

Take It Further 3

▶ 1H Take It Further 3 (CD: 1, Track: 9)

One of the most distinctive features of Russian phonetics is the phenomenon called "palatalization" or "softness." It occurs when the articulation of a consonant slightly shifts upward and to the front of your mouth, that is, toward the hard palate; hence, the term. As a result, the consonant sounds somewhat "softer." When this happens in English, it usually goes unnoticed since "soft" and "hard" consonants don't differentiate meaning but rather reflect regional or personal accents. In Russian, the distinction is fully meaningful.

Now, let's look at all of the Russian consonants from the standpoint of their "softness/hardness." Three consonants in Russian are always "hard," i.e., they cannot be palatalized; they are ж [zh], ш [sh], and ц [ts]. For example,

ж—госпожа́ [gəs-pah-ZHAH], журнали́стка [zhur-nah-LEEST-kə], пожа́луйста [pah-ZHAH-lə-stə]

ш—хорошо́ [hə-rah-SHOH], ц—америка́нец [ah-mi-ri-KAH-nits], царь [TSAHR'] (*tsar*).

Two consonants and one semi-vowel or glide are always "soft," that is to say, palatalized. They are щ [shch], ч [ch], й [y or i – as in boy]. For example,

щ—щи [SHCHEE] (*cabbage soup*), това́рищ [tah-VAH-rishch] (*comrade*), ве́щи [VEH-shchee] (*things*)

ч—о́чень [AW-chin'], ве́чер [VEH-chir] (*evening*)
й—зра́вствуйте [ZDRAH-stvəi-ti], пойдёмте [pahi-DʲOM-ti]

The remaining fifteen consonants—Б б, В в, Г г, Д д, З з, К к, Л л, М м, Н н, П п, Р р, С с, Т т, Ф ф, Х х—can be either soft or hard, depending on their position in the word. Having a separate letter for each one of them would have made the Russian alphabet longer by fifteen letters, which, of course, would not have been practical. Thus, two other simple methods solved the problem for these consonants.

If one of these fifteen consonants is followed by the mute soft sign ь, it is soft! E.g., мать [MAT'] means *mother* when the т is soft; but when the т is hard, as in мат [MAT], it means *mate* (as in checkmate). The phonetic distinction between the soft т and the hard т may appear subtle to the non-Slavic ear, but it is of paramount importance in Russian. Be patient and try to attune your ear to it! Here are more examples of soft consonants softened by the soft sign from your vocabulary lists: о́чень прия́тно [AW-chin' pri-YAT-nə]; добро́ пожа́ловать [dah-BRAW pah-ZHAH-lə-vət']. Notice that, in our phonetic transcription, an apostrophe after such a consonant marks its softness.

If one of the fifteen "palatalizable" consonants is followed by one of the five "soft" vowels я, ю, е, ё, and и it is also soft! For example, лук [LOOK– with a hard л] means *onion*, but люк [L'OOK – with a soft л] means *trapdoor*. Here are more examples already familiar to you (the underlined consonants are made soft by the following "soft vowels": америка́нец [ah-mi-ri-KAH-nits], господи́н [gəs-pah-DEEN], приве́т [pri-V'ET], пойдёмте [pahy-D'OM-ti].

When you first hear the difference, it may appear to you that there is a brief [i] sound between the soft consonant and the following soft vowel. While the [i] is in fact not really there, imagining it there may help you make the distinction. Consequently, we use a small ' in our transcription to mark the softness of such consonants.

If one of these fifteen consonants is not followed by the soft sign ь or by any of the "soft" vowels, it is "hard." As you might guess, the five "hard" vowels (а, у, э, о, and ы) don't palatalize the preceding consonant either; it remains "hard." For example, in the words госпо́ди́н [gəs-pah-DEEN], спаси́бо [spah-SEE-bə], прия́тно [pri-IAHT-nə], the underlined consonants are normal, that is to say, hard.

✎ Work Out 2
▶ 1I Work Out 2 (CD: 1, Track: 10)

A. Which form of greeting would you use when greeting the following people? When choosing among здра́вствуй, здра́вствуйте, and приве́т, be aware of the formal/informal and singular/plural distinctions.

1. *a police officer* _Здравствуйте_

2. *a child* _Здравствуй_ _Привет_

3. *a classmate at school* _Привет_

4. *a waiter* _Здравствуйте_

5. *two students* _Здравствуйте_

6. *schoolchildren* _Здравствуй_

7. *a business partner at a formal meeting* _Здравствуйте_

8. *your sister* _Привет_

B. What form of *excuse me* (извини́ or извини́те) would you use while apologizing to the following people?

1. *a passenger on a train* _Извините_

2. *a mother and a child on a train* _Извините_

3. *a child* _Извини_

4. *your spouse* _Извините_

5. *a shop assistant* _Извините_

6. *your childhood friend* _Извини_

7. *your grandfather* _Извини_

8. *two children* _Извините_ ←?

C. Now let's do some audio exercises. Listen to the audio and give the English equivalents to the Russian expressions.

1. Как дела? _How are you_

2. Вы говорите по-русски? _Do you speak Russian?_

3. Я студентка. _I am a student (F)_

4. Пойдёмте. _Let's go!_

5. Пожалуйста. _Please / You're welcome_

6. Очень приятно. _Good to meet you_

7. Добро пожаловать! _Welcome_

8. Спасибо. _Thank you_

9. До свидания. _Goodbye (formal)_

10. Я американец. _I am american (M)_

D. Give Russian equivalents to the following English expressions.

1. *Hello, gentlemen!* _Здравствуйте Господа_
2. *Good-bye, Mrs. Smirnova.* _До свидания, Госпожа_
3. *Thank you!* _Спасиба_
4. *Let's go, Mr. Smith.* _Пойдёмте Господин Смит_
5. *How are you?* _Как дела_
6. *Please.* _Пожалуйста_
7. *Welcome!* _Доброе Пожалветь Пожаловать_
8. *Do you speak Russian?* _Вы говорите по-русски?_
9. *A little bit.* _Немного_
10. *Nice to meet you.* _Очень приятно приятно_

ANSWER KEY

A. 1. здра́вствуйте; 2. здра́вствуй, приве́т; 3. приве́т; 4. здра́вствуйте; 5. здра́вствуйте;
6. здра́вствуйте; 7. здра́вствуйте; 8. здра́вствуй, приве́т

B. 1. извини́те; 2. извини́те; 3. извини́; 4. извини́; 5. извини́те; 6. извини́; 7. извини́; 8. извини́те

C. 1. *How are you?* 2. *Do you speak Russian?* 3. *I am a student.* 4. *Let's go!* 5. *Please.* 6. *Nice to meet you.*
7. *Welcome!* 8. *Thank you.* 9. *Good-bye.* 10. *I am an American.*

D. 1. Здра́вствуйте, господа́! 2. До свида́ния, госпожа́ Смирно́ва. 3. Спаси́бо! 4. Пойдёмте,
господи́н Смит. 5. Как дела́? 6. Пожа́луйста. 7. Добро́ пожа́ловать! 8. Вы говори́те по-ру́сски?
9. Немно́го. 10. О́чень прия́тно.

✎ Drive It Home

A. What gender is each of the following nouns? Replace them with the appropriate
third person pronoun—он, она́, or они́.

1. господи́н _ОН_

2. америка́нец _ОН_

3. журнали́ст _он_

4. студе́нт _он_

5. Джон _он_

6. америка́нка _она_

7. журнали́стка _она_

8. студе́нтка _она_

9. госпожа́ _она_

10. Ири́на _она_

11. америка́нец и америка́нка _они_

12. господа́ _они х ачи_

13. Джон и Ири́на _они_

B. Which Russian pronoun would you use when addressing the following people? There are two second person pronouns to choose from: ты, informal for one person, and вы, formal for one person and either formal or informal for more than one person.

1. *a child* _ты_

2. *your sister* _ты_

3. *your grandmother* _ты_

4. *your father* _ты_

5. *a police officer* _вы_

6. *a waiter* _вы_

7. *two children* _вы_

8. *your parents* Вы

9. *your brothers* Вы

10. *two students* Вы

ANSWER KEY

A. 1. он; 2. он; 3. он; 4. он; 5. он; 6. она; 7. она; 8. она; 9. она; 10. она; 11 они; 12. они; 13. они
B. 1. ты; 2. ты; 3. ты; 4. ты; 5. вы; 6. вы; 7. вы; 8. вы; 9. вы; 10. вы

Take It Further 4

Did you notice in the above dialogue that the question Вы говори́те по-
ру́сски? [vy gə-vah-REE-ti pah-ROOS-ki] (*Do you speak Russian?*) is identical to
the statement Вы (хорошо́) говори́те по-ру́сски [vy hə-rah-SHOH gə-vah-REE-ti
pah-ROOS-ki] (*You speak Russian [well]*)? This is because all yes or no questions
are grammatically identical to their affirmative statement counterparts. The only
difference is the intonation. To make an affirmative sentence into a question, just
raise your tone in the stressed syllable of the word in question. For example, here
the word in question is говори́те because you want to know whether the person
speaks Russian or not (rather than whether the person speaks Russian or French).
Therefore, the tone of your voice should sharply go up within the space of the и
in говори́те while the rest of the sentence, including the other three syllables of
the word in question, will more or less remain at a middle tone. Although such
an abrupt change in intonation may at first sound unnatural to you, it's perfectly
normal and emotionally neutral in Russian.

Parting Words

Well done! You've completed the first lesson of Essential Russian! By now, you should be able to:

☐ Greet someone and ask how they're doing. (Still unsure? Go back to page 11.)

☐ Use basic courtesy expressions. (Still unsure? Go back to page 11.)

☐ Ask simple questions when you meet someone. (Still unsure? Go back to page 11.)

☐ Recognize masculine and feminine nouns. (Still unsure? Go back to page 13.)

☐ Use both formal and informal forms of address. (Still unsure? Go back to page 16.)

Don't forget to practice and reinforce what you've learned by visiting **www.livinglanguage.com/ languagelab** for flashcards, games, and quizzes!

Lesson 2: People and Family

Второ́й уро́к: Лю́ди и семья́

[ftah-ROI oo-RAWK LʲOO-dee i sʲee-MYAH]

Добро́ пожа́ловать, ещё раз! *Welcome once again!* Are you ready for a new challenge? In this lesson, you'll learn how to:

☐ Talk about your immediate family.

☐ Recognize gender in Russian.

☐ Talk about your extended family.

Once again, we'll start with some vocabulary building. You'll hear the English first, and then you'll hear the Russian. Repeat each new phrase every time you hear it. Let's begin!

Vocabulary Builder 1

▶ 2A Vocabulary Builder 1 (CD: 1, Track: 11)

family	семья *(always fem. sg.)*	sⁱee-MIAH
mother, mom	мать, ма́ма	MAHT', MAH-mah
father, dad	оте́ц, па́па	ah-TⁱETS, PAH-pah
son	сын	SYN
daughter (inform.)	дочь, до́чка	DAWCH, DAWCH-kə
brother	брат	BRAHT
sister	сестра́	sⁱee-STRAH
grandmother	ба́бушка	BAH-bush-kə
grandfather	де́душка	DⁱE-dush-kə
parents	роди́тели	rah-DEE-ti-li
children	де́ти	DⁱE-tee

✎ Vocabulary Practice 1

Now, let's review the new words. Match the English words on the left with their Russian equivalents on the right.

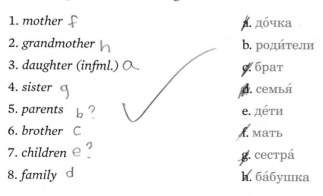

1. *mother* f
2. *grandmother* h
3. *daughter (infml.)* a
4. *sister* g
5. *parents* b ?
6. *brother* c
7. *children* e ?
8. *family* d

a. до́чка
b. роди́тели
c. брат
d. семья́
e. де́ти
f. мать
g. сестра́
h. ба́бушка

ANSWER KEY
1. f; 2. h; 3. a; 4. g; 5. b; 6. c; 7. e; 8. d

Grammar Builder 1

▶ 2B Grammar Builder 1 (CD: 1, Track: 12)

DISTINGUISHING MASCULINE AND FEMININE NOUNS

As you learned in Lesson 1, all Russian nouns have gender. The gender of the nouns for human beings is obvious—those referring to males are masculine, to females, feminine. The gender of nouns referring to inanimate objects is determined by their endings. For now, we'll deal only with masculine and feminine nouns referring to human beings and will look at masculine, feminine, and neuter nouns referring to objects in a later lesson.

As a rule, masculine nouns end in a consonant, for example, отéц (*father*), брат (*brother*); however, there's a significant group of masculine nouns that end in an а or я, such as пáпа (*dad*), дéдушка (*grandfather*), Вáня (*Vanya*).

Most feminine nouns end in a vowel а or я, such as мáма (*mom*), семья́ (*family*), бáбушка (*grandmother*); however, there's a group of feminine nouns that end in the soft sign, for example, мать (*mother*). In the future, we will call this group of feminine nouns "the soft sign feminines."

Vocabulary Builder 2

▶ 2C Vocabulary Builder 2 (CD: 1, Track: 13)

boy	мáльчик	MAHL'-chik
girl (preadolescent)	дéвочка	DⁱE-vəch-kə
young man	молодóй человéк	mə-lah-DOI chi-lah-VⁱEK
young lady, girlfriend, partner	дéвушка	DⁱE-vahsh-kə
friend (male)	друг	DROOK

friend (female), girlfriend	подру́га	pahd-ROO-gə
husband	муж	MOOZH
wife	жена́	zhi-NAH
my (sg. masc.)	мой	MOI
my (sg. fem.)	моя́	mah-IAH
my (pl.)	мои́	mah-IEE
This is … /These are …	Э́то …	EH-tə
man, a male	мужчи́на	muhsh-CHEE-nə
woman, a female	же́нщина	ZHEN-shchi-nə

Take It Further 1

Notice that the Russian equivalent of *my* (also known as the first person singular possessive pronoun) changes, according to the gender of the nouns it modifies. Therefore, the masculine form мой will be coupled with singular masculine nouns (мой муж /*my husband*), the feminine моя́ will be coupled with feminine nouns (моя́ жена́ /*my wife*), and the plural мои́ with plural nouns (мои́ де́ти /*my children*).

✎ Vocabulary Practice 2

A. Write the noun that is appropriate to the gender and number of the possessive pronouns below.

1. мой   *Друг*

   male friend

2. мой   *Муж*

   husband

3. мой _Маладой Челофек_

young man

X 4. мой _Пата Отец_

father

5. мой _Дедуша отец_

grandfather

6. моя _Девочка_

girl

7. моя _жена_

wife

8. моя _бабушка_

grandmother

9. моя _Девушка_

girlfriend

10. моя _Семья Семья_

family

11. мой _Дети_

children

12. мой _родители_

parents

B. Now do the opposite and write the possessive pronoun *my*—мой (*sg. masc.*), моя (*sg. fem.*), мои (*pl.*)—appropriate to the gender and number of the nouns it modifies.

1. X~~Моя~~ Мой _____ друг

2. Мой _____ ма́льчик

3. Мой _____ муж

4. X~~Моя~~ Мой _____ де́душка

5. Мой _____ молодо́й челове́к

6. Моя _____ жена́

7. Моя _____ де́вушка

8. Моя _____ ба́бушка

9. X~~Мой~~ Моя _____ подру́га

10. Моя _____ де́вочка

11. Мои _____ де́ти

12. Мои _____ роди́тели

Answer Key

A. 1. друг; 2. муж; 3. молодо́й челове́к; 4. оте́ц; 5. де́душка; 6. де́вочка; 7. жена́; 8. ба́бушка; 9. де́вушка; 10. семья́; 11. де́ти; 12. роди́тели

B. 1. мой; 2. мой; 3. мой; 4. мой; 5. мой; 6. моя́; 7. моя́; 8. моя́; 9. моя́; 10. моя́; 11. мой; 12. мой

Grammar Builder 2

▶ 2D Grammar Builder 2 (CD: 1, Track: 14)

INTRODUCING PEOPLE OR THINGS WITH ЭТО

When you first introduce a person—or show a thing—you use a construction that is simpler in Russian than it is in English. All you do is this: you just say Это (*this/these*) and then mention the person or thing you introduce.

This is my friend.	Это мой друг.	EH-tə MOI DROOK
These are my children.	Это мои дети.	EH-tə mah-EE DⁱE-tee
This is my wife.	Это моя жена́.	EH-tə mah-IAH zhi-NAH
This is John.	Это Джон.	EH-tə DZHAWN

Notice that, unlike English, the Russian demonstrative pronoun это always stays the same whether it introduces a singular or plural noun; and the verb *to be*, as you already know, is omitted in the present tense in Russian.

When you want to refer to someone or something mentioned earlier, you use one of the regular pronouns он, она́, оно́ (neuter pronoun), or они́ depending on the gender and number of the noun you are referring to by the pronoun.

| This is John. He is my friend. | Это Джон. Он мой друг. | EH-tə DZHAWN AWN MOI DROOK |
| This is my daughter. She is a student. | Это моя́ дочь. Она́ студе́нтка. | EH-tə mah-IAH DAWCH ah-NAH stoo-DⁱENT-kə |

As explained in Lesson 1, you can easily turn the above statements into questions just by raising your intonation. For example,

| Is this John? | Это Джон? | EH-tə DZHAWN |
| Yes, this is John. | Да, это Джон. | DAH EH-tə DZHAWN |

✎ Work Out 1

▶ 2E Work Out 1 (CD: 1, Track: 15)

Let's review. As in the previous lesson, listen to the audio and fill in the missing words. Repeat the correct answers in the pauses provided for practice.

1. *This is my family—my wife, my daughter, and my son.*

   Это ___моя___ семья— ___моя___ женá, ___моя___ дочь и ___мой___ сын.

2. *This is Mr. Bill Turner. He is a businessman and my friend.*

   ___Это___ господи́н Билл Тёрнер. ___Он___ бизнесме́н и мой ___друг___.

3. *Natasha is a girl.*

   Натáша ___девочка___.

4. *Vanya is a boy.*

   Вáня ___мальчик___. мальчик

5. *These are my children, Natasha and Vanya.*

   Это ___мои___, Натáша и Вáня.

6. *Excuse me, young man!*

   Извини́те, ___молодой человек___

7. *Excuse me, young lady!*

   Извини́те, ___девушка___!

8. *This is my husband, John.*

   Это ___мой муж___ Джон.

9. *This is my girlfriend.*

   Это ___моя___ подру́га.

10. *This is my brother.*

Э́то мои́ брáт.

11. *Mr. Turner is a man.*

Господи́н Тёрнер мужчина. *мужчина*

12. *Mrs. Turner is a woman.*

Госпожá Тёрнер женщина. *женщина*

ANSWER KEY
1. моя́, моя́, моя́, мой; 2. Э́то, Óн, друг; 3. дéвочка; 4. мáльчик; 5. мои́ дéти; 6. молодóй человéк;
7. дéвушка; 8. мой муж; 9. Э́то моя́; 10. Э́то мой; 11. мужчи́на; 12. жéнщина

Bring It All Together
▶ 2F Bring It All Together (CD: 1, Track: 16)

Now let's bring it all together with a dialogue. Let's listen to Bill talk to Olya about a photograph of his family.

Olya:	*Excuse me, Bill. Is this your photograph?*
Оля:	Извини́те, Билл. Э́то вáша фотогрáфия?
	[iz-vi-NEE-ti BIL eh-TAH VAH-shə fə-tə-GRAH-fi-iah]
Bill:	*Yes, it's mine. This is my family and I (lit. I and my family)*
Билл:	Да, моя́. Э́то я и моя́ семья́.
	[DAH mə-IAH eh-TAH IA I mə-IAH sʲee-MIAH]
Olya:	*Tell me please, is this your wife?*
Óля:	Скажи́те, пожáлуйста, э́то вáша женá?
	[skah-ZHEE-ti pah-ZHAH-lahs-tə eh-TAH VAH-shə zhi-NAH]
Bill:	*Yes, this is my wife, Stephanie. She is a journalist.*
Билл:	Да, э́то моя́ женá, Стéфани. Онá журнали́стка.
	[DAH eh-TAH mah-IAH zhi-NAH STE-fə-nee ah-NAH zhur-nah-LEEST-kə]
Olya:	*And are these your children?*
Óля:	А э́то вáши дéти?

[ah-EH-tə VAH-shi DⁱEH-ti]

Bill:	*Yes, these are my children; a boy and a girl.*
Билл:	Да, э́то мои́ де́ти, ма́льчик и де́вочка.

[DAH EH-tə mah-IEE DⁱEH-ti MAHL'chik i DⁱEE-vəch-kə]

Olya:	*And what are their names?*
О́ля:	А как их зову́т?

[ah KAHK ikh-zah VOOT]

Bill:	*The boy is Tom and the girl is Lisa. They are students.*
Билл:	Ма́льчик—Том, а де́вочка—Ли́за. Они́ студе́нты.

[MAHL'-chik TAWM ah-DⁱEE-vəch-kə LEE-zə ah-NEE stuh-DⁱEHN-ty]

Olya:	*And is this your father and your mother?*
Оля:	А э́то ваш оте́ц и ва́ша мать?

[ah-EH-tə VASH ah-TⁱEHTS i-VAH-shə MAHT']

Bill:	*Yes, these are my parents, (my) mother and father.*
Билл:	Да, э́то мои́ роди́тели, мать и оте́ц.

[DAH EH-tə mah-IEE rah-DEE-ti-li MAT' I ah-TⁱEHTS]

Olya:	*Very interesting.*
О́ля:	О́чень интере́сно.

[AW-chin' in-tee-RⁱEHS-nə]

Take It Further 2

▶ 2G Take It Further 2 (CD: 1, Track: 17)

As you have probably noticed from the dialogue above, the Russian forms of the
formal *your*—just like the forms of *my* мой, моя́, мои́—also agree with the nouns
they modify. They have the same set of endings—what's called a "zero" ending for
masculine pronouns, an –а for feminine, and an –и for plurals. For example:

ваш оте́ц (*masc.*)	*your father*
ва́ша ма́ма/мать (*fem.*)	*your mom/mother*
ва́ши де́ти (*pl.*)	*your children*

The noun фотогра́фия [fə-tah-GRAH-fi-iə] is a cognate, or a word that sounds just like its English equivalent; it means *photograph*.

Кто [KTAW] is a question word meaning *who*. When you use it with э́то , as in Кто э́то? [KTAW-əh-tə], it means, *Who is this?* or *Who are they?*

Also, notice the conjunction а [AH]. It can be roughly translated as *and* although it really doesn't have a precise equivalent in English and in fact stands for something between the English *and* and *but*. Oftentimes, it introduces a new item within the old context. For example, in a conversation about one's family (the old context), when you move to a new family member (the new item), you preface your "move" with an а :

| *This is my wife. And this is my son.* | Это моя́ жена́. А э́то мой сын. | eh-TAH mah-IAH zhi-NAH ah-EH-tə MOI SYN |

And finally, скажи́те ,пожа́луйста , [skah-ZHEE-ti pah-ZHAH-luhi-stə] is a common phrase used with requests for information. It literally means *tell me please* and is the plural or formal form; if you're talking to just one person you know well, you'd use the informal скажи́ ,пожа́луйста , [skah-ZHEE pah-ZHAH-luhi-stə]. Notice that пожа́луйста (*please*) is always written between commas in Russian.

✎ Work Out 2

A. Fill in the blanks with the correct form of the possessive pronoun *my*—мой ,моя́ , or мой —and then read the sentences out loud. The translations are provided to help you.

1. Это ___мой___ сын.

   This is my son.

2. Это _мой_ муж.

   This is my husband.

3. Это _моя_ студе́нтка.

   This is my female student.

4. Это _моя_ ба́бушка.

   This is my grandmother.

5. Это _моя_ жена́.

   This is my wife.

6. Это _моя_ дочь.

   This is my daughter.

7. Это _моя_ фотогра́фия.

   This is my photograph.

8. Это _моя_ семья́.

   This is my family.

9. Это _мои_ роди́тели.

   These are my parents.

10. Это _мои_ де́ти.

    These are my children.

B. Now, insert the nouns to match the given possessive pronouns.

1. Это мой _муж_

   This is my husband.

2. Это мой _семья сын_

This is my son.

3. Это моя _студентка_

This is my female student.

4. Это моя _семья_

This is my family.

5. Это моя _бабушка_

This is my grandmother.

6. Это моя _жена_

This is my wife.

7. Это моя _дочь_

This is my daughter.

8. Это моя _Фотография_

This is my photograph.

9. Это мой _дети_

These are my children.

10. Это мой _родители_

These are my parents.

ANSWER KEY

A. 1. мой; 2. мой; 3. моя; 4. моя; 5. мой; 6. моя; 7. моя; 8. моя; 9. мой; 10. мой
B. 1. муж; 2. сын; 3. студе́нтка; 4. семья́; 5. ба́бушка; 6. жена́; 7. дочь/до́чка; 8. фотогра́фия;
9. де́ти; 10. роди́тели

✎ Drive It Home

It's time for another Drive It Home section designed to make using the structures you've learned more automatic. Remember that, even though these exercises may seem simple and repetitive, they reinforce your understanding of the subject and make you accustomed to the sounds and grammatical structures of Russian. Make sure you spend some time with them, write out each exercise completely, and say the answers aloud.

A. First, let's round up some of the masculine nouns you've learned so far. Fill in the blanks with the correct nouns and their possessive pronoun мой following the prompts in the parentheses.

1. Это _____. (my boy)

2. Это _____. (my young man)

3. Это _____. (my male friend)

4. Это _____. (my husband)

5. Это _____. (my father)

6. Это _____. (my son)

7. Это _____. (my brother)

8. Это _____. (my grandfather)

B. Now, let's do the same for the feminine nouns and their possessive pronoun моя.

1. Это _____. (my girl)

2. Это _____. (my young lady/girlfriend)

3. Это _____. (my female friend/girlfriend)

4. Это _____.(*my wife*)

5. Это _____.(*my family*)

6. Это _____.(*my mother*)

7. Это _____.(*my daughter*)

8. Это _____.(*my sister*)

9. Это _____.(*my grandmother*)

10. Это _____.(*my photograph*)

C. And finally, let's do the plurals and their possessive pronoun мои́

1. Это _____.(*my parents*)

2. Это _____.(*my children*)

ANSWER KEY
A. 1. мой ма́льчик 2. мой молодо́й челове́к 3. мой друг 4. мой муж 5. мой оте́ц 6. мой сын
7. мой брат 8. мой де́душка
B. 1. моя́ де́вочка 2. моя́ де́вушка 3. моя́ подру́га 4. моя́ жена́ 5. моя́ семья́ 6. моя́ мать 7. моя́
дочь/до́чка 8. моя́ сестра́ 9. моя́ ба́бушка 10. моя́ фотогра́фия
C. 1. мои́ роди́тели 2. мои́ де́ти

Take It Further 3
▶ 2H Take It Further 3 (CD: 1, Track: 18)

Remember for future use that Russian also has nouns that are neuter. Most of
them end in either an o or e Consequently, their possessive pronouns would also
end in a e or ё For example, the noun вино́ [vee-NAW] (*wine*) is neuter, so you'd
say моё вино́ [mah-IAW vee-NAW] (*my wine*) and ва́ше вино́ [VAH-shə vee-NAW]
(*your wine*). All plural forms in Russian are "gender blind."

As mentioned in Lesson 1, most Russian consonants can be either hard or soft
even though they are spelled with the same letter. One consonant, however, is an

exception: its "soft" and "hard" variants each have a letter and thus remain always hard or soft respectively. The always-soft consonant is Щ щ[shch]. Remember, when it's spelled "with a tail," it's soft. Without the "tail"—as a Ш ш[sh], it's always hard. The phonetic difference may appear very subtle to you, but to the Russian ear it is unmistakable. For example, the шin ши́на[SHEE-nə] (tire) and на́ши[NAH-shee] (our) is different from the щin щи[SHCHEE] (cabbage soup) and о́вощи[AW-və-shchee] (vegetables). You'll see the difference marked in the phonetics in this book as [sh] for Ш шand [shch] for Щ щ

Parting Words

Well done! After this lesson, you should be able to:

☐ Talk about your immediate family. (Still unsure? Go back to page 31.)

☐ Recognize gender in Russian. (Still unsure? Go back to page 32.)

☐ Talk about your extended family. (Still unsure? Go back to page 32.)

Don't forget to practice and reinforce what you've learned by visiting **www.livinglanguage.com/ languagelab** for flashcards, games, and quizzes!

Word Recall

Let's review some of the key vocabulary you've learned in these two lessons. Remember that this is an opportunity to review the words and structures that we've covered so far so that you can retain them in your long-term memory for future use.

Fill in the following family tree with the correct Russian words for each member of the family. Make sure to include the appropriate possessive pronoun for each of your family members.

1. _____ (Father)
2. _____ (Mother)
3. _____ (Sister)
   you
4. _____ (Brother)

Now, tell us something about them. Translate the following sentences into Russian.

1. *Hello! Are you Mr. Smith? Nice to meet you!*

_____

2. *My father is a businessman. He is an American.*

_____

3. *My mother is a journalist. She is Russian.*

_____

4. *This is my brother, John. He is a student.*

_____

5. *Is this your daughter? Is she a student?*

_____

6. *This is my family—my wife, my parents, and my children.*

_____

ANSWER KEY
1. Здра́вствуйте! Вы господи́н Смит? О́чень прия́тно! 2. Мой оте́ц – бизнесме́н. Он америка́нец. 3. Моя́ мать – журнали́стка. Она́ ру́сская. 4. Э́то мой брат Джон. Он студе́нт. 5. Э́то ва́ша дочь? Она́ студе́нтка? 6. Э́то моя́ семья́ – моя́ жена́, мои́ роди́тели и мои́ де́ти.

Lesson 3: Around the Home

Тре́тий уро́к: Дома́
[TRʲE-ti-i oo-RAWK: DAW-mə]

Добро́ пожа́ловать, ещё раз! *Welcome once again!* In Lesson 3, you'll learn how to:

☐ Use the numeral *one* in Russian.

☐ Recognize neuter nouns in Russian.

☐ Use plurals for the basic types of Russian nouns.

☐ Ask to whom a thing or things belong.

Let's get started! By now, you know that you'll hear the English followed by the Russian. Repeat each new word or phrase every time you hear it.

Vocabulary Builder 1

▶ 3A Vocabulary Builder 1 (CD: 1, Track: 19)

one (masc. sg.)	оди́н	ah-DEEN
one (fem. sg.)	одна́	ah-DNAH
one (neuter sg.)	одно́	ah-DNAW
one, nobody but, alone (pl.)	одни́	ah-DNEE
it (neuter sg.)	оно́	ah-NAW
table, desk	стол (masc.)	STAWL
chair	стул (masc.)	STOOL
house, home	дом (masc.)	DAWM
apartment	кварти́ра (fem.)	kvahr-TEE-rə
room	ко́мната (fem.)	KAWM-nə-tə
thing	вещь (fem.)	VⁱEHSHCH
wine	вино́ (neuter)	vee-NAW
window	окно́ (neuter)	ahk-NAW
letter	письмо́ (neuter)	pees'-MAW
sea	мо́ре (neuter)	MAW-rⁱə

Take It Further 1

▶ 3B Take It Further 1 (CD: 1, Track: 20)

There are three genders in Russian. In addition to masculine and feminine nouns, there are some neuter nouns. Masculine and feminine nouns can denote people or things. Neuter nouns denote things only. There's no apparent reason why one inanimate noun is masculine, feminine, or neuter. This is a purely grammatical property which should be memorized and, most of the time, in accordance with their endings. For example, вино́[vee-NAW] (wine), окно́[ahk-NAW] (window), письмо́[pees'-MAW] (letter), мо́ре[MAW-rⁱə] (sea) are all neuter nouns. As such, they are modified by the neuter forms of одно́ [ah-DNAW] (*one*) and моё [mah-YAW] (*my*) and replaced by the neuter pronoun оно́ [ah-NAW] (*it*). For example, you'd say

одно́ вино́
one wine

моё вино́
my wine

Э́то вино́. Оно́ моё.
This is wine. It is mine.

одно́ окно́
one window

моё окно́
my window

Э́то окно́. Оно́ моё.
This is a window. It is mine.

одно́ письмо́
one letter

моё письмо́
my letter

Э́то письмо́. Оно́ моё.
This is a letter. It is mine.

✎ Vocabulary Practice 1

Match the English words in the left column with the Russian equivalents on the right. Say the Russian words out loud.

1. *apartment*   n ✓   а. одна́
2. *it (neuter)*   l ✓   b. ко́мната
3. *sea*   k ✓   c. дом
4. *window*   i ✓   d. стол
5. *letter*   h ✓   e. оди́н   *один*
6. *house*   c ✓   f. вино́
7. *chair*   m ✓   g. одни́
8. *table*   d ✓   h. письмо́   *одно*
9. *wine*   f. ✓   i. окно́
10. *room*   b ✓   j. одно́
11. *one (masc. sg.)*   e ✓   k. мо́ре
12. *one (fem. sg.)*   a ✓   l. оно́
13. *one (neut. sg.)*   j   m. стул
14. *one/alone (pl.)*   g   n. кварти́ра

ANSWER KEY

1. n; 2. l; 3. k; 4. i; 5. h; 6. c; 7. m; 8. d; 9. f; 10. b; 11. e; 12. a; 13. j; 14. g

Grammar Builder 1

▶ 3C Grammar Builder 1 (CD: 1, Track: 21)

EXPRESSIONS WITH THE NUMERAL ONE

The numeral *one* has gender in Russian, which means that it matches the gender of the nouns it modifies. For example, if it's modifying a masculine noun, it's in the masculine form.

оди́н америка́нец
[ah-DEEN ah-mi-ri-KAH-nits]
one [male] American

оди́н стул
[ah-DEEN STOOL]
one chair

If it's modifying a feminine noun, it's in the feminine form.

одна́ вещь
[ah-DNAH VⁱEHSHCH]
one thing

одна́ кварти́ра
[ah-DNAH kvahr-TEE-rə]
one apartment

If it's modifying a neuter noun, it's neuter.
одно́ письмо́
[ah-DNAW pees'-MAW]
one letter

одно́ окно́
[ah-DNAW ahk-NAW]
one window

In the plural form, одни́ this numeral means *alone* or *nobody but*. For example,

одни́ дети́[ah-DNEE DⁱEH-ti] means *only children* or *nobody but children*;
одни́ роди́тели [ah-DNEE rah-DEE-ti-li] means *only parents* or *nobody but parents*.

However, if you switch around the numeral *one* and the noun it modifies, the phrase also changes its meaning to *"X is one/alone"* or *"XX are alone."* For instance,

Мой сын оди́н.

[MOI SYN ah-DEEN]

My son is alone.

Моя́ дочь одна́.

[mah-YAH DAWCH ah-DNAH]

My daughter is alone.

Мои́ роди́тели одни́.

[mah-EE rah-DEE-ti-li ah-DNEE]

My parents are alone.

Vocabulary Builder 2

▶ 3D Vocabulary Builder 2 (CD: 1, Track: 22)

whose (masc. sg.)	чей	CHEI
whose (fem. sg.)	чья	CHYAH
whose (neut. sg.)	чьё	CHYAW
whose (pl.)	чьи	CHYEE
tables	столы́	stah-LY
rooms	ко́мнаты	KAWM-nə-ty
apartments	кварти́ры	kvahr-TEE-ry
photographs	фотогра́фии	fə-tah-GRAH-fi-i
things	ве́щи	VⁱEH-shchi
houses, homes	дома́	dah-MAH

people, persons	лю́ди	L'OO-di
windows	о́кна	AWK-nə
wines	ви́на	VEE-nə
seas	моря́	mah-R'AH
Americans	америка́нцы	ah-mi-ri-KAHN-tsy
students	студе́нты	stu-D'EHN-ty
friends	друзья́	dru-ZYAH

Take It Further 2

The ending –ы or –и makes most Russian nouns plural. Notice how оди́н сто́л (*one table*) became столы́ (*tables*) in the plural, одна́ кварти́ра (*apartment*) became кварти́ры (*apartments*), оди́н америка́нец (*one American*) became америка́нцы (*Americans*), фотогра́фия (*photograph*) became фотогра́фии (*photographs*), вещь (*thing*) became ве́щи (*things*), etc. However, neuter nouns normally have an –a for the plural ending and two syllable neuter nouns usually shift the stress from one syllable to the other. For example, окно́ (*window*) becomes о́кна (*windows*) in the plural, вино́ (*wine*) becomes ви́на (*wines*), and мо́ре (*sea*) becomes моря́ (*seas*). In addition, some plurals are irregular and need to be memorized. For example, дом (*house, home*)—which is a masculine, not neuter, noun—forms the plural with an –a ending, дома́ (*houses*); and друг (*friend*) is друзья́ (*friends*) in the plural.

✎ Vocabulary Practice 2

Form plurals from the following singular nouns and repeat them out loud. Pay
attention to the correct endings and stress shifts.

1. стол _____

2. стул _____

3. студе́нт _____

4. америка́нец _____

5. ко́мната _____

6. кварти́ра _____

7. вещь _____

8. студе́нтка _____

9. америка́нка _____

10. фотогра́фия _____

11. окно́ _____

12. письмо́ _____

13. вино́ _____

14. друг _____

15. дом _____

ANSWER KEY
1. столы́; 2. сту́лья; 3. студе́нты; 4. америка́нцы; 5. ко́мнаты; 6. кварти́ры; 7. ве́щи; 8. студе́нтки;
9. америка́нки; 10. фотогра́фии; 11. о́кна; 12. пи́сьма; 13. ви́на; 14 друзья́; 15. дома́

Grammar Builder 2

▶ 3E Grammar Builder 2 (CD: 1, Track: 23)

ASKING WHOSE IN RUSSIAN

The question word *whose* also has gender and number in Russian, that is to say, it agrees in gender and number with the noun it modifies. For example, if you're asking about a male person or a masculine object, you'd use the masculine singular form of *whose*— чей, a female person or a feminine object, you'd use the feminine singular form of *whose*— чья, a neuter object, you'd use the neuter form of *whose*— чьё, and if you're asking about anyone or anything in the plural form, you'd use a plural form of *whose*— чьи

Чей э́то сын?
Whose son is this?

Чей э́то дом?
Whose house is this?

Чья э́то дочь?
Whose daughter is this?

Чья э́то кварти́ра?
Whose apartment is this?

Чьё э́то окно́?
Whose window is this?

Чьё э́то письмо́?
Whose letter is this?

Чьи э́то ве́щи?

Whose things are these?

Чьи э́то фотогра́фии?

Whose photographs are these?

✎ Work Out 1

▶ 3F Work Out 1 (CD: 1, Track: 24)

Now, let's review. As always, listen to the audio and fill in the missing words. Repeat the correct answers in the pauses provided for practice.

1. *This is one house.*

   Э́то оди́н _____.

2. *This is one table.*

   Э́то оди́н _____.

3. *Whose chair is this?*

   Чей э́то _____?

4. *This is one room.*

   Э́то одна́ _____.

5. *This is one apartment.*

   Э́то одна́ _____.

6. *Whose photograph is this?*

   Чья э́то _____?

7. *This is one window.*

   Э́то одно́ _____.

8. *This is one letter.*

   Э́то одно́ _____.

9. *Whose wine is this?*

   Чьё э́то _____?

10. *Whose parents are they?*

    Чьи э́то _____?

11. *Whose friends are they?*

    Чьи э́то _____?

12. *Whose letters are these?*

    Чьи э́то _____?

13. *Whose things are these?*

    Чьи э́то _____?

ANSWER KEY
1. дом; 2. стол; 3. стул; 4. ко́мната; 5. кварти́ра; 6. фотогра́фия; 7. окно́; 8. письмо́; 9. вино́;
10. роди́тели; 11. друзья́; 12. пи́сьма; 13. ве́щи

Bring It All Together
▶ 3G Bring It All Together (CD: 1, Track: 25)

Now let's bring it all together with a dialogue. Let's listen to this conversation
between Jack and Lena about Jack's belongings.

Lena:	*Excuse me please, whose room is this?*

Лена:	Извини́те, пожа́луйста, чья э́то ко́мната?
	[iz-vi-NEE-ti pah-ZHAH-ləs-tə CHYAH EH-tə KAWM-nə-tə]
Jack:	*This is my room.*
Джек:	Э́то моя́ ко́мната.
	[EH-tə mah-YAH KAWM-nə-tə]
Lena:	*And whose desk is this?*
Лена:	А чей э́то стол?
	[ah-CHEY EH-tə STAWL]
Jack:	*This is my desk.*
Джек:	Э́то мой стол.
	[EH-tə MOI STAWL]
Lena:	*And whose chair is this?*
Лена:	А чей э́то стул?
	[ah-CHEI EH-tə STOOL]
Jack:	*This is also my chair.*
Джек:	Э́то то́же мой стул.
	[EH-tə TAW-zhə MOI STOOL]
Lena:	*And whose letters are these? Are these your letters?*
Лена:	А чьи э́то пи́сьма? Э́то ва́ши пи́сьма?
	[ah-CHYEE EH-tə PEES'-mə EH-tə VAH-shi PEES'-mə]
Jack:	*Yes, these are my things—my letters and photographs.*
Джек:	Да, э́то мои́ ве́щи—мои́ пи́сьма и фотогра́фии.
	[DAH EH-tə mah-EE V'EH-shchi mah-EE PEES'-mə i-fə-tah-GRAH-fi-i]
Lena:	*Do you live here alone [lit.: one]?*
Лена:	Вы здесь живёте оди́н?
	[VY-zd'is' zhy-V'AW-ti ah-DEEN]
Jack:	*Yes, I live here alone.*
Джек:	Да, я здесь живу́ оди́н.
	[DAH YAH-zd'is' zhy-VUH ah-DEEN]

Lena:	And who are you?
Лёна:	А кто вы?
	[ah-KTAW-vy]
Jack:	I am a student. I am an American. My name is Jack and this is my house/home.
Джек:	Я студе́нт. Я америка́нец. Меня́ зову́т Джек, и э́то мой дом.
	[YAH stuh-DⁱEHNT YAH ah-mi-ri-KAH-nits mi-NⁱAH zah-VUHT DZHEHK i-EH-tə MOI DAWM]

Take It Further 3

You must have noticed two personal pronouns я [YAH] (*I*) and вы [VY] (*you*). Two things to note about these pronouns are, first, я is not capitalized in Russian unless it occurs in the beginning of the sentence. Also, ты is informal singular and вы can be formal and singular or plural (informal or formal), much like the archaic English *thou* which was informal singular and *you* which was formal singular or plural (informal or formal).

These pronouns are followed by the appropriate forms of the verb *to live*: я живу́ and вы живёте.

You'll learn personal pronouns and basic forms of verbal conjugation in the following chapter. For now, just remember how they are used in a sentence.

✎ Work Out 2

▶ 3H Work Out 2 (CD: 1, Track 26)

A. Fill in the blanks with the correct form of the question word *whose*—чей ,чья ,
чьё , orчьи —and then read the sentences out loud. The translations are provided
to help you.

1. *Whose house is this?*

   _____ э́то дом?

2. *Whose table/desk is this?*

   _____ э́то стол?

3. *Whose chair is this?*

   _____ э́то стул?

4. *Whose student is this?*

   _____ э́то студе́нт?

5. *Whose son is this?*

   _____ э́то сын?

6. *Whose apartment is this?*

   _____ э́то кварти́ра?

7. *Whose room is this?*

   _____ э́то ко́мната?

8. *Whose [female] student is this?*

   _____ э́то студе́нтка?

9. *Whose photograph is this?*

_____ э́то фотогра́фия?

10. *Whose daughter is this?*

_____ э́то дочь?

11. *Whose letter is this?*

_____ э́то письмо́?

12. *Whose window is this?*

_____ э́то окно́?

13. *Whose wine is this?*

_____ э́то вино́?

14. *Whose things are these?*

_____ э́то ве́щи?

15. *Whose photographs are these?*

_____ э́то фотогра́фии?

B. When you hear a phrase in Russian, please translate it into English.

1. оди́н дом _____

2. оди́н друг _____

3. оди́н стол _____

4. оди́н стул _____

5. одна́ кварти́ра _____

6. одна́ ко́мната _____

7. одна́ студе́нтка _____

8. одна́ америка́нка _____

9. одно́ окно́ _____

10. одно́ мо́ре _____

11. одно́ вино́ _____

12. одни́ друзья́ _____

13. одни́ дома́ _____

14. одни́ де́ти _____

C. Now, give the Russian equivalent to the English phrase you'll hear.

1. *Whose house is this?* _____

2. *Whose desk is this?* _____

3. *Whose apartment is this?* _____

4. *Whose room is this?* _____

5. *Whose wine is this?* _____

6. *Whose letter is this?* _____

7. *Whose children are they?* _____

8. *Whose things are these?* _____

9. *These are my things.* _____

10. *This is one letter.* _____

11. *This is my room.* _____

12. *This is my desk.* _____

ANSWER KEY

A. 1. Чей ; 2. Чей ; 3. Чей ; 4. Чей ; 5. Чей ; 6. Чья ; 7. Чья ; 8. Чья ; 9. Чья ; 10. Чья ; 11. Чьё ; 12. Чьё ; 13. Чьё ; 14. Чьи ; 15. Чьи

B. 1. *one house*; 2. *one friend*; 3. *one desk/table*; 4. *one chair*; 5. *one apartment*; 6. *one room*; 7. *one (female) student*; 8. *one (female) American*; 9. *one window*; 10. *one sea*; 11. *one wine*; 12. *only friends*; 13. *only houses*; 14. *only children*

C. 1. Чей э́то дом? 2. Чей э́то стол? 3. Чья э́то кварти́ра? 4. Чья э́то ко́мната? 5. Чьё э́то вино́? 6. Чьё э́то письмо́? 7. Чьи э́то де́ти? 8. Чьи э́то ве́щи? 9. Э́то мои́ ве́щи. 10. Э́то одно́ письмо́. 11. Э́то моя́ ко́мната. 12. Э́то мой стол.

✎ Drive It Home

Now, let's wrap everything up with another Drive It Home section. Make sure you spend some time with the sentences here, write out each exercise completely, and say the answers aloud!

A. First, use the appropriate masculine singular form to modify the following masculine singular nouns.

1. _____ э́то дом. (*whose*)

   Э́то _____ дом. (*my*)

   Э́то _____ дом. (*one*)

2. _____ э́то друг? (*whose*)

   Э́то _____ друг. (*my*)

   Э́то _____ друг. (*one*)

3. _____ э́то стул? (*whose*)

   Э́то _____ стул. (*my*)

   Э́то _____ стул. (*one*)

B. Then, use the appropriate feminine singular form to modify the following feminine singular nouns.

1. _____ э́то ко́мната? (whose)

   Э́то _____ ко́мната. (my)

   Э́то _____ ко́мната. (one)

2. _____ э́то фотогра́фия? (whose)

   Э́то _____ фотогра́фия. (my)

   Э́то _____ фотогра́фия. (one)

3. _____ э́то кварти́ра? (whose)

   Э́то _____ кварти́ра. (my)

   Э́то _____ кварти́ра. (one)

C. Now, use the appropriate neuter singular form to modify the following neuter singular nouns.

1. _____ э́то окно́? (whose)

   Э́то _____ окно́. (my)

   Э́то _____ окно́. (one)

2. _____ э́то вино́? (whose)

   Э́то _____ вино́. (my)

   Э́то _____ вино́. (one)

3. _____ э́то письмо́? (whose)

   Э́то _____ письмо́. (my)

   Э́то _____ одно́. (one)

D. And finally, use the appropriate plural form to modify the following plural nouns.

1. _____ э́то дома́? (*whose*)

   Э́то _____ дома́. (*my*)

2. _____ э́то друзья́? (*whose*)

   Э́то _____ друзья́. (*my*)

3. _____ э́то лю́ди? (*whose*)

   Э́то _____ лю́ди. (*my*)

ANSWER KEY
A. 1. Чей, мой, оди́н; 2. Чей, мой, оди́н; 3. Чей, мой, оди́н
B. 1. Чья, моя́, одна́; 2. Чья, моя́, одна́; 3. Чья, моя́, одна́
C. 1. Чьё, моё, одно́; 2. Чьё, моё, одно́; 3. Чьё, моё, одно́
D. 1. Чьи, мои́, одни́; 2. Чьи, мои́, одни́; 3. Чьи, мои́, одни́

Take It Further 4

Remember the sentence Меня́ зову́т Джек [mi-N'AH zah-VUHT DZHEHK] (*My name is Jack*.) from the dialogue above? This simple English phrase, *My name is X*, is more complicated in Russian. Its literal translation is *Me [they] call X*. You'll understand its grammar when you learn the conjugation of verbs and the accusative case of pronouns and nouns in the later chapters. For now, once again, memorize this phrase as it is, but keep in mind that you can use it only for *my name* (not for *your name, his name*, etc.).

Parting Words

Congratulations! You've completed another lesson of *Essential Russian*. In this lesson you learned how to:

☐ Use the numeral *one* in Russian. (Still unsure? Go back to page 49.)

☐ Recognize neuter nouns in Russian. (Still unsure? Go back to page 49.)

☐ Use plurals for the basic types of Russian nouns. (Still unsure? Go back to page 53.)

☐ Ask to whom a thing or things belong. (Still unsure? Go back to page 56.)

Don't forget to practice and reinforce what you've learned by visiting **www.livinglanguage.com/languagelab** for flashcards, games, and quizzes!

Word Recall

Let's review some of the key vocabulary you've learned in these three lessons. Remember that this is an opportunity to review the words and structures that we've covered so far so that you can retain them in your long-term memory for future use.

A. What would the following phrases be in the plural form?

1. мой стол _____

2. мой друг _____

3. мой стул _____

4. моя́ фотогра́фия _____

5. моя́ студе́нтка _____

6. моя́ ко́мната _____

7. моё окно́ _____

8. моё вино́ _____

9. моё письмо́ _____

B. Fill in the blanks with the missing Russian word.

1. Э́то мой _____. (friends)

   Они́ _____. (Americans)

2. Э́то мой _____. (house)

   Я здесь живу́ _____. (alone/one)

3. Э́то моя́ _____: мой _____ и _____. (*family, parents, children*)

4. _____, вы журнали́ст? (*Excuse me please*)

5. _____ Тёрнер—америка́нский _____. (*Mr., businessman*)

_____ _____ говори́т по-ру́сски. (*He, well*)

Lesson 4: Locations

Четвёртый уро́к: Местоположе́ния
[cheht-VⁱAWR-tyi oo-ROK: mⁱeh-stə-pə-lah-ZHE-ni-yə]

Добро́ пожа́ловать, ещё раз! *Welcome once again!* In this fourth lesson, you'll learn some basic expressions and other useful words, phrases, and grammar points to get you started speaking Russian. You'll learn how to:

☐ Speak about the location of a person or thing.

☐ Use the prepositions в and на.

☐ Use basic nouns in the prepositional case.

☐ Speak about rooms and furniture in an apartment.

☐ Put it all together in a simple conversation.

But let's begin with the new words and phrases. As usual, you'll hear the English words first, and then you'll hear the Russian words, which you should repeat every time you hear them. Ready?

Vocabulary Builder 1

4A Vocabulary Builder 1 (CD: 1, Track: 27)

in (at, on)	в	v *or* f
on (at, in)	на	nah *or* nə
in the apartment	в кварти́ре	fkvahr-TEE-ri
at the hotel	в гости́нице	vgahs-TEE-ni-tsi
in the room	в ко́мнате	FKAWM-nə-ti
in the kitchen	на ку́хне	nah-KOOH-ni
on the table	на столе́	nə-stah-LⁱEH
in the dining room/dining hall	в столо́вой	vstah-LAW-vəy
at/in the restaurant	в рестора́не	vri-stah-RAH-ni
in the café	в кафе́	fkah-FEH
street	у́лица	OO-li-tsə
in/on the street	на у́лице	nah-OO-li-tsi
in Russia	в Росси́и	vrah-SEE-i
in America	в Аме́рике	vah-MⁱEH-ri-ki
in the picture	на фотогра́фии	nə-fə-tah-GRAH-fi-i

Take It Further 1

4B Take It Further 1 (CD: 1, Track: 28)

THE PREPOSITIONS В AND НА

There are two basic prepositions in Russian that denote locations—в and на. Generally speaking, в, means *in* and на means *on*. However, there's no precise correspondence between the English and Russian prepositions expressing locations and every now and then the English *on* (or *at*) will be translated as the Russian в and the English *in* (or *at*) as the Russian на. Rather than equating

Lesson 4: Locations   71

Russian prepositions with English ones, you need to learn them in connection with the specific nouns and just remember them as a pair. Just to appreciate this inter-linguistic mismatch, consider the following examples

at school
в шко́ле
[f-SHKAW-li]*on the train*
в по́езде
[f-PAW-iz-di] *in the picture*
на фотогра́фии
[nə-fə-tah-GRAH-fi-i]

Vocabulary Practice 1

Are you ready for practice? Match the English in the left column with the Russian in the opposite column.

1. *in the apartment*   a. на у́лице
2. *on the table*   b. на фотогра́фии
3. *street*   c. в столо́вой
4. *at the restaurant*   d. на ку́хне
5. *in Russia*   e. на столе́
6. *in/on the street*   f. в Аме́рике
7. *in America*   g. в кварти́ре
8. *in the photograph*   h. в Росси́и
9. *in the kitchen*   i. в рестора́не
10. *in the dining room*   j. у́лица

ANSWER KEY
1. g; 2. e; 3. j; 4. i; 5. h; 6 .a; 7. f; 8. b; 9. d; 10. c

Grammar Builder 1

▶ 4C Grammar Builder 1 (CD: 1, Track: 29)

THE PREPOSITIONAL CASE

You must have noticed that most Russian nouns have an additional ending –е when they indicate locations of other people or things. This ending marks what is called prepositional case. It replaces the standard noun ending –а or it's simply added to the last consonant of the standard noun ("zero ending"). For example,

стол—на столе́	on the table
ресторан—в рестора́не	in the restaurant
квартира—в кварти́ре	in the apartment
кухня—на ку́хне	in the kitchen

By way of exception, some nouns will have an –ии ending in the prepositional case. These nouns have a penultimate (second to last) letter –и–. For example, many countries ending in –ия belong to this category.

Russia–in Russia	Росси́я—в Росси́и	rah-SEE-yə – vrah-SEE-i
Italy–in Italy	Ита́лия—в Ита́лии	i-TAH-li-yə – vy-TAH-li-i
Germany–in Germany	Герма́ния—в Герма́нии	gir-MAH-ni-yə – vgir-MAH-ni-i
England–in England	А́нглия—в А́нглии	AHN-gli-yə – VAHN-gli-i

And so, you've just had your first introduction to Russian cases and learned the prepositional case!

In Russian, as well as in Greek and Latin, a case simply refers to a change in a noun's (pronoun's or adjective's) ending when it plays different roles in a sentence. For example, this can be the role of the subject (the nominative case), a stationary location (the prepositional case), direct object (the accusative case), a place one moves to as opposed to a stationary location (again the accusative case), a topic of a conversation or thought (again the prepositional case but with another preposition), and so on. Including the nominative case—which is the "original" case of a noun as it's listed in a dictionary—there are six cases in Russian. The number of "roles" nouns can play in a sentence is much greater; therefore, several "roles" or "functions" can be covered by one case. For now, we'll focus only on the "locative function/role" of the prepositional case.

Take It Further 2

The phrase в столо́вой (*in the dining room* or *in the dining hall/cafeteria*) has a different ending because it is an adjective that functions as a noun, a so-called "substantivized adjective," much like the English word "patient" (*He is patient.* v. *He is a patient.*). If you remember this ending, you'll know the prepositional case of Russian feminine adjectives. The nouns, ва́нная [VAH-nə-yə] (*bathroom*) and гости́ная [gahs-TEE-nə-yə] (*living room*), are also substantivized adjectives; since they modify the implied feminine noun ко́мната (*room*), they are feminine as well.

Vocabulary Builder 2

(▶) 4D Vocabulary Builder 2 (CD: 1, Track: 30)

where	где	GD\u2071EH
in the living room	в гости́ной	vgahs-TEE-nəy
in the bathroom	в ва́нной	VVAHN-əy
bathroom, restroom, toilet	туале́т	too-ah-L\u2071EHt
in the restroom	в туале́те	ftoo-ah-L\u2071EH-ti
closet	шкаф	SHKAHF
in the closet	в шкафу́	fshkah-FOO

floor	пол	PAWL
on the floor	на полу́	nə-pah-LOO
corner	у́гол	OO-gəl
in the corner [of a room]	в углу́	voo-GLOO
armchair	кре́сло	KRⁱEHS-lə
in the armchair, on the armchair	в кре́сле, на кре́сле	FKRⁱEHS-li nahKRⁱEHS-li
in the chair	на сту́ле	nah-STOO-li
bed, in bed, on the bed	крова́ть, в крова́ти, на крова́ти	krah-VAHT' vkrah-VAH-ti nə-krah-VAH-ti
bedroom	спа́льня	SPAHL'-nⁱə
in the bedroom	в спа́льне	FSPAHL'-ni
couch	дива́н	di-VAHN
on the couch	на дива́не	nə-di-VAH-ni

✎ Vocabulary Practice 2

What's wrong with the following statements? Consider the corrections suggested in the parentheses and choose one that fits best.

1. Стол на дива́не? Нет, он _____. (в туале́те, в ва́нной, на полу́)

2. Крова́ть в столо́вой? Нет, она́ _____. (на сту́ле, в спа́льне, в шкафу́)

3. Стул в туале́те? Нет, он _____. (в столо́вой, в крова́ти, на дива́не)

4. Шкаф в кре́сле? Нет, он _____. (на у́лице, в углу́, на крова́ти)

5. Дива́н в шкафу́? Нет, он _____ . (в ко́мнате, в кре́сле, в

ва́нной)

ANSWER KEY
1. на полу́; 2. в спа́льне; 3. в столо́вой; 4. в углу́; 5. в ко́мнате

Grammar Builder 2

▶ 4E Grammar Builder 2 (CD: 1, Track: 31)

ASKING *WHERE* IN RUSSIAN

The question word где? (*where?*) asks about a location of a person or thing.
Unlike the question word *whose* (чей, чья, чьё, чьи), it always stays the same.
The location it asks about requires the prepositional case. So you can associate
this case with the question где. Also remember for future use, that *where* in
Russian is different from *where to*. We call this distinction "location vs. direction."

Since the verb *to be* is omitted in the present tense, the English construction *there
is/there are* consists just of the item/items that is/are and the place where they
are. For example, you should translate the sentence *There is a table in the kitchen*
into Russian as

Стол на ку́хне.
or
На ку́хне стол.

Old (i.e. already discussed) information usually comes first in Russian sentences,
so the difference between them is this:

Стол на ку́хне. (We've been talking about the table located in the kitchen.)
vs.
На ку́хне стол. (We've been talking about the kitchen, which has a table.)

Take It Further 3

Notice two other exceptional groups of nouns that take an ending other than
–e in the prepositional case. A small group of one-syllable masculine nouns will
have a stressed –у to mark a location, e.g., на полу́ (*on the floor*), в шкафу́ (*in the
closet*); and soft sign feminine nouns will have an –и in the prepositional case, e.g.,
в кровати́ (*in bed*).

✎ Work Out 1

▶ 4F Work Out 1 (CD: 1, Track: 32)

Let's review. As usual, listen to the audio first and then fill in the missing Russian
words. Finally, repeat the correct answers in the pauses provided for practice.
Remember that the verb *to be* is omitted in the present tense in Russian.

1. *There is a kitchen, a living room, and a bedroom in the apartment.*

   В кварти́ре _____, _____, и _____.

2. *There's a window in the bathroom.*

   _____ окно́.

3. *There are windows in the kitchen.*

   _____ о́кна.

4. *There is a closet and a bed in the bedroom.*

   В спа́льне _____ и _____.

5. *Where is your son? He is in bed.*

   Где ваш сын? Он _____.

6. *Where is the bed? It's in the bedroom.*

   Где крова́ть? Она́ _____.

7. *The armchair is in the corner.*

   Кре́сло _____.

8. *My things are on the floor.*

   Мои́ ве́щи _____.

9. *Where's your wife? She's in America.*

   Где ва́ша жена́? Она́ _____.

10. *Where's your husband? He's in Russia.*

    Где ваш муж? Он _____.

ANSWER KEY
1. ку́хня, гости́ная, спа́льня; 2. В ва́нной; 3. На ку́хне; 4. Шкаф, крова́ть; 5. в крова́ти;
6. в спа́льне; 7. в углу́; 8. на полу́; 9. в Аме́рике; 10. в Росси́и

Bring It All Together
▶ 4G Bring It All Together (CD: 1, Track: 33)

Now let's bring it all together, and add a little more vocabulary and structure.
Listen to Oleg showing Olga his apartment.

Oleg: *Hello, Olga! This is my apartment. Welcome!*
Оле́г: Здра́вствуй, О́льга! Э́то моя́ кварти́ра. Добро́ пожа́ловать!
          [ZDRAH-stvəy AWL'-gə EH-tə mah-YAH kvahr-TEE-rə dahb-RAW pah-
          ZHAH-lə-vət']

Olga: *Hello, Oleg! Thank you.*
О́льга: Здра́вствуй, Оле́г. Спаси́бо.
          [ZDRAH-stvəy ah-LⁱEHK spah-SEE-bə]

Oleg: *Here's the living room and the dining room.*

Олег:	Вот э́то гости́ная и столо́вая.
	[vawt-EH-tə gah-STEE-nə-yə i-stah-LAW-və-yə]
Olga:	*And where's the kitchen?*
Ольга :	А где ку́хня?
	[ah-GDⁱEH KOOH-nⁱə]
Oleg:	*Over there. There's a table in the kitchen.*
Олег:	Вон там. На ку́хне стол.
	[vawn-TAHM nah-KOOH-ni STAWL]
Olga:	*And where's the bathroom and toilet?*
Ольга:	А где ва́нная и туале́т?
	[ah-GDⁱEH VAHN-ə-yə i-tuh-ah-LⁱEHT]
Oleg:	*They are there, where the bedroom is.*
Олег:	Они́ там, где спа́льня.
	[ah-NEE TAHM gdi-SPAHL'-nⁱə]
Olga:	*Is the closet there too?*
Ольга:	А шкаф то́же там?
	[ah-SHKAHF TAW-zhi-tahm]
Oleg:	*Yes, it's in the bedroom.*
Олег:	Да, шкаф в спа́льне.
	[DAH SHKAHF FSPAHL'ni]
Olga:	*And where's the couch?*
Ольга:	А где дива́н?
	[ah-GDⁱEH di-VAHN]
Oleg:	*The couch is in the living room.*
Олег:	Дива́н в гости́ной.
	[di-VAHN vgah-STEEN-əy]
Olga:	*This is a very good apartment!*
Ольга:	Э́то о́чень хоро́шая кварти́ра!
	[EH-tə AW-chin' hah-RAW-shy-yə kvahr-TEE-rə]
Oleg:	*Thank you, Olga!*
Олег:	Спаси́бо, Ольга!
	[spah-SEE-bə AWL'-gə]

Lesson 4: Locations   79

Take It Further 4

It's hard to give good English equivalents to the Russian words вот and вон used in this dialogue and yet they are quite common in Russian speech. Вот means *here* except that it's used in constructions similar to *Here it is* rather than *It's here*; it points something out rather than stating that something is nearby. Вон has the same demonstrative function but it points something out far away; it's often followed by the adverb там (*there*) and roughly translates as *over there*. For example,

Вот моя́ кварти́ра.
Here's my apartment.

Вон там мой дом.
My house is over there.

Work Out 2

▶ 4H Work Out 2 (CD: 1, Track: 34)

Answer the following questions using the prompts in parentheses.

A.

1. Где фотогра́фия?

   Она́ _____. (*on the table*)

2. А где стол?

   Он _____. (*in the living room*)

3. А где гости́ная?

   Она́ _____. (*in the apartment*)

4. А где кварти́ра?

   Она́ _____. (in America)

B.

1. Где туале́т?

   Он _____. (in the restaurant)

2. Где крова́ть?

   Она́ _____. (in the bedroom)

3. Где кре́сло?

   Оно́ _____. (in the corner)

4. Где ваш муж?

   Он _____. (in the street)

5. Где ва́ши де́ти?

   Они́ _____. (in Russia)

6. Где кафе́?

   Оно́ _____ (at the hotel)

C. Listen to the following phrases in Russian, repeat them in Russian aloud, and then translate into English.

1. в ко́мнате _____

2. в кварти́ре _____

3. в рестора́не _____

4. на у́лице _____

5. на фотогра́фии _____

D. Now, listen to the following phrases in English, provide Russian equivalents, and practice saying them aloud.

1. *in Russia* _____

2. *in America* _____

3. *in the corner* _____

4. *on the couch* _____

5. *in the armchair* _____

ANSWER KEY

A. 1. на столе́; 2. в гости́ной; 3. в кварти́ре; 4. в Аме́рике

B. 1. в рестора́не; 2. в спа́льне; 3. в углу́; 4. на у́лице; 5. в Росси́и; 6. в гости́нице

C. 1. *in the room*; 2. *in the apartment*; 3. *in the restaurant*; 4. *in the street*; 5. *in the photograph*

D. 1. в Росси́и; 2. в Аме́рике; 3. в углу́; 4. на дива́не; 5. в кре́сле

✎ Drive It Home

Now, ask and answer a question about the location of a person or thing stated in the sentences below. Remember to substitute a third person pronoun for the person or thing in question. Follow this example:

The table is in the kitchen.

Стол на ку́хне.

_____

_____

You say: Где стол? Он на ку́хне.

Where's the table? It's in the kitchen.

1. Крова́ть в спа́льне.

   _____

   _____

2. Стул на ку́хне.

   _____

   _____

3. Америка́нец в Росси́и.

   _____

   _____

4. Ве́щи на полу́.

   _____

   _____

5. Кре́сло в углу́.

   _____

   _____

6. Сын в крова́ти.

   _____

   _____

7. Студе́нты в столо́вой.

   _____

   _____

8. Бизнесме́н в гости́нице.

_____

_____

ANSWER KEY

1. Где крова́ть? Она́ в спа́льне. 2. Где стул? Он на ку́хне. 3. Где америка́нец? Он в Росси́и. 4. Где ве́щи? Они́ на полу́. 5. Где кре́сло? Оно́ в углу́. 6. Где сын? Он в крова́ти. 7. Где студе́нты? Они́ в столо́вой. 8. Где бизнесме́н? Он в гости́нице.

Take It Further 5

▶ 4I Take It Further 5 (CD: 1, Track: 35)

You've learned many of the words you need to describe your apartment and locate people and things. Here are a few more useful "locations":

When someone or something is *at home,* you should use a special form of the noun дом (*house, home*)—до́ма—without prepositions or case endings. For example, you should just say:

Моя́ жена́ до́ма.
My wife is at home.

Мои́ де́ти до́ма.
My children are at home.

Мои́ ве́щи до́ма.
My things are at home.

When someone or something is *at work,* you should use the standard prepositional case of the feminine noun рабо́та (*work*) along with the preposition на—на рабо́те (*at work*). By the way, the English word *robot* is a borrowing from another Slavic language, Czech, which is closely related to Russian. Use this connection as a mnemonic device!

Мой брат на рабóте.
My brother is at work.

Эта фотогрáфия на рабóте.
That photograph is at work.

Parting Words

By now you should know how to:

☐ Speak about the location of a person or thing. (Still unsure? Go back to page 71.)

☐ Use the prepositions в and на. (Still unsure? Go back to page 71.)

☐ Speak about rooms and furniture in an apartment. (Still unsure? Go back to page 74.)

☐ Use basic nouns in the prepositional case. (Still unsure? Go back to page 73.)

☐ Put it all together in a simple conversation. (Still unsure? Go back to page 78.)

Don't forget to practice and reinforce what you've learned by visiting **www.livinglanguage.com/languagelab** for flashcards, games, and quizzes!

Word Recall

Let's review some of the key vocabulary you've learned in these four lessons. Fill in the blanks with the correct Russian translations of the following phrases.

1. *window* _____

2. *a little bit* _____

3. *apartment* _____

4. *sea* _____

5. *one letter* _____

6. *husband* _____

7. *wife* _____

8. *This is my friend.* _____

9. *in Russia* _____

10. *on the floor* _____

ANSWER KEY
1. окно́; 2. Немно́го.; 3. кварти́ра; 4. мо́ре; 5. одно́ письмо́; 6. муж 7. жена́; 8. Э́то мой друг.; 9. в Росси́и; 10. на полу́

Essential Russian

Lesson 5: Everyday Life

Пя́тый уро́к: Где вы живёте?
[PʲAH-tyi oo-ROK: GDʲEH-vy zhi-VʲAW-ti]

Здра́вствуйте и ещё раз добро́ пожа́ловать! *Hello and welcome once again!*
In this fifth lesson, you'll learn how to:

☐ Talk about where one resides and works.

☐ Use Russian personal pronouns.

☐ Conjugate basic Russian verbs.

☐ Discuss basic daily meals.

☐ Refer to different times of day using appropriate time expressions.

☐ Put it all together in a simple conversation.

Let's begin by looking at two verbs and their forms in the present tense. These
will be the verbs жить [ZHYTʲ] (*to live, to reside, to stay [e.g., in a hotel]*) and
рабо́тать [rah-BAW-tətʲ] (*to work*). You're already familiar with some of the
personal pronouns; the chart below will provide you with the entire set of them.
As always, you'll hear the English first, and then you'll hear the Russian. Repeat
each new word or phrase every time you hear it.

Гото́вы? [gah-TAW-vy] (*Ready?*)

Vocabulary Builder 1

▶ 5A Vocabulary Builder 1 (CD: 2, Track: 1)

I live	я живу́	YAH zhi-VOO
you (inform. sg.) live	ты живёшь	TY zhi-VⁱAWSH
he, she lives	он, она́ живёт	AWN ah-NAH zhi-VⁱAWT
we live	мы живём	MY zhi-VⁱAWM
you (form. sg. or pl.) live	вы живёте	VY zhi-VⁱAW-ti
they live	они́ живу́т	ah-NEE zhi-VⁱOOT
I work	я рабо́таю	YAH rah-BAW-tə-yu
you (inform. sg.) work	ты рабо́таешь	TY rah-BAW-tə-yish
he, she works	он, она́ рабо́тает	AWN ah-NAH rah-BAW-tə-yit
we work	мы рабо́таем	MY rah-BAW-tə-yim
you (form. sg. or pl.) work	вы рабо́таете	VY rah-BAW-tə-yi-ti
they work	они́ рабо́тают	ah-NEE rah-BAW-tə-yuht

✎ Vocabulary Practice 1

Let's practice what you've just learned!

A. First, fill in the blanks with the appropriate personal pronoun. Remember that the verbs жить (to live) and рабо́тать (to work) take the prepositional case expressing a stationary location.____ живу́ в Аме́рике._____ живём в Аме́рике._____ живёшь в Аме́рике._____ живёте в Аме́рике._____ _____ живёт в Аме́рике._____ живу́т в Аме́рике.____ рабо́таю в Росси́и.

1. _____ рабо́тает в Росси́и.

2. _____ рабо́таете в Росси́и.

3. _____ рабо́таешь в Росси́и.

4. _____ рабо́таем в Росси́и.

5. _____ рабо́тают в Росси́и.

6. _____ рабо́тает в Росси́и.

B. Now, fill in the blanks with the appropriate form of the verbs жить (1–7) and рабо́тать (8–13) matching the given pronoun.

1. Я _____ в Росси́и.

2. Он _____ в Росси́и.

3. Вы _____ в Росси́и.

4. Ты _____ в Росси́и.

5. Мы _____ в Росси́и.

6. Они́ _____ в Росси́и.

7. Она́ _____ в Росси́и.

8. Я _____ в Аме́рике.

9. Он _____ в Аме́рике.

10. Вы _____ в Аме́рике.

11. Ты _____ в Аме́рике.

12. Мы _____ в Аме́рике.

13. Они́ _____ в Аме́рике.

Lesson 5: Everyday Life   **89**

14. Она́ _____ в Аме́рике.

ANSWER KEY

A. 1. Я; 2. Мы; 3. Ты; 4. Вы; 5. Он/она́; 6. Они́; 7. Я; 8. Он/она́; 9. Вы; 10; Ты; 11. Мы; 12. Они́;
13. Он/она́

B. 1. живу́; 2. живёт; 3. живёте; 4. живёшь; 5. живём; 6. живу́т; 7. живёт; 8. рабо́таю; 9. рабо́тает;
10. рабо́таете; 11. рабо́таешь; 12. рабо́таем; 13. рабо́тают; 14. рабо́тает

Grammar Builder 1

▶ 5B Grammar Builder 1 (CD: 2, Track: 2)

INTRODUCTION TO CONJUGATION TYPES

There are two basic conjugation types in Russian. The verb жить (*to live*) belongs
to Type I. The standard endings for this type are:

SINGULAR	PLURAL
–у/–ю	–ем (–ём)
–ешь (–ёшь)	–ете (–ёте)
–ет (–ёт)	–ут/–ют

The choice between –у or –ю depends on whether the stem of the verb ends in a
hard consonant (then it takes a hard ending –у) or soft (then it has a soft ending
–ю). If the verb ending happens to be stressed, then the –e becomes –ё.

The standard infinitive ending is –ть in Russian. It has the same function as the
English particle *to* before verbs. So *to live* equals жить.

Type II conjugation is almost exactly the same except that the –e (–ё) of Type I
is replaced by an –и and the third person plural endings are –ат/–ят in Type II
conjugation.

SINGULAR	PLURAL
–у/–ю	–им
–ишь	–ите

SINGULAR	PLURAL
–ит	–ат/–ят

The verb говори́ть [gə-vah-RIT'] *to speak, to talk* has Type II conjugation. This is how it changes for different persons.

SINGULAR	PLURAL
я говорю́	мы говори́м
ты говори́шь	вы говори́те
он/она́ говори́т	они́ говоря́т

There can also be minor and generally predictable changes within the stem of the conjugated verb, which we call mutations. And of course, there are some verbs that are exceptions. We'll introduce Type II verbs, as well as verbs with mutations and other exceptions later on. The good news, however, is that Russian has only these two types of conjugations you'll have to memorize—that's all!

Vocabulary Builder 2

▶ 5C Vocabulary Builder 2 (CD: 2, Track: 3)

at home	до́ма	DAW-mə
at work	на рабо́те	nə-rah-BAW-ti
office, in the office	о́фис, в о́фисе	AW-fis, VAW-fi-si
firm, company at the firm/company	фи́рма, на фи́рме	FEER-mə, nah-FEER-mi
to have breakfast	за́втракать	ZAHF-trə-kət'
to have lunch	обе́дать	ah-BⁱEH-dət'
to have dinner/supper	у́жинать	UH-zhi-nət'
in the morning	у́тром	UHT-rəm
in the afternoon	днём	DNⁱAWM

in the evening	вéчером	VᶦEH-chi-rəm
sometimes	иногдá	i-nah-GDAH
often	чáсто	CHAHS-tə
always	всегдá	fsig-DAH

✎ Vocabulary Practice 2

A. Now it's time to put the vocabulary and grammar you've just learned to work. Choose the correct pronoun for the verbs below. Repeat the complete sentence out loud.

1. Утром _____ зáвтракаю дóма.

2. Утром _____ зáвтракаешь дóма.

3. Утром _____ зáвтракает дóма.

4. Утром _____ зáвтракаем дóма.

5. Утром _____ зáвтракаете дóма.

6. Утром _____ зáвтракают дóма.

B.

1. Днём _____ обéдаю на рабóте.

2. Днём _____ обéдаешь на рабóте.

3. Днём _____ обéдает на рабóте.

4. Днём _____ обéдаем на рабóте.

5. Днём _____ обéдаете на рабóте.

6. Днём _____ обéдают на рабóте.

C.

1. Вéчером _____ ýжинаю в ресторáне.

2. Вéчером _____ ýжинаешь в ресторáне.

3. Вéчером _____ ýжинает в ресторáне.

4. Вéчером _____ ýжинаем в ресторáне.

5. Вéчером _____ ýжинаете в ресторáне.

6. Вéчером _____ ýжинают в ресторáне.

ANSWER KEY
A. 1. я; 2. ты; 3. он/онá; 4. мы; 5. вы; 6. онѝ
B. 1. я; 2. ты; 3. он/онá; 4. мы; 5. вы; 6. онѝ
C. 1. я; 2. ты;. 3. он/онá; 4. мы; 5. вы; 6. онѝ

Grammar Builder 2

▶ 5D Grammar Builder 2 (CD: 2, Track: 4)

TALKING ABOUT DAILY MEALS

The verbs рабóтать (*to work*), зáвтракать (*to have breakfast*), обéдать (*to have lunch*), and ýжинать (*to have dinner/supper*)—all belong to the same conjugation type and all have the same type of endings. All of them also take the prepositional case, that is to say, they are often followed by a noun in the prepositional case that indicates a location where one works, has breakfast, lunch, or dinner.

Just like the time expressions иногдá (*sometimes*), чáсто (*often*), всегдá (*always*), the words ýтром, днём, and вéчером are adverbs. Their meaning is equivalent to the English *in the morning, in the afternoon*, and *in the evening/tonight/at night* (if "night" stands for the time when people go out, not the time when people are normally asleep). Notice that these Russian time expressions, as opposed to their English equivalents, don't have prepositions!

The Russian word дóма means *at home* and you also need to use it without a preposition.

✎ Work Out 1

▶ 5E Work Out 1 (CD: 2, Track: 5)

Now that you've learned some new words and expressions that describe what you do in the course of a day, let's see how they fit together. Listen to the audio first, then fill in the missing Russian words, and finally, repeat the correct answers in the pauses provided. Note that expressions like *in the morning, in the afternoon, at home*, etc. are never followed by a comma in Russian when they are in the beginning of the sentence.

1. *In the morning, I have breakfast at home.*

   Утром я зáвтракаю_____.

2. *In the afternoon, I work in the office.*

   _____я рабóтаю в óфисе.

3. *In the evening, she works at home.*

   Вéчером онá_____ дóма.

4. *Sometimes, I have lunch in the afternoon.*

   Иногдá я_____ днём.

5. *Sometimes, I have dinner in the evening at a restaurant.*

   _____я ýжинаю вéчером в ресторáне.

6. *I often work at home(from home).*

   Я ча́сто _____ до́ма.

7. *Where do you (form.) live?*

   Где вы _____ ?

8. *They live in America.*

   Они́ живу́т_____ .

9. *Sometimes, he works in Russia.*

   Иногда́ он_____ в Росси́и.

10. *Sometimes, we have lunch in a café.*

    Иногда́ мы_____ в кафе́.

   ANSWER KEY
   1. до́ма; 2. днём; 3. рабо́тает; 4. обе́даю; 5. Иногда́; 6. рабо́таю; 7. живёте; 8. в Аме́рике;
   9. рабо́тает; 10. обе́даем

Bring It All Together

▶ 5F Bring It All Together (CD: 2, Track: 6)

Now let's listen to a dialogue that brings together everything you've learned in
this lesson. Jennifer is asking Nikolai, who is temporarily in America on business,
about his daily routine. Remember to repeat the Russian sentences in the pauses
provided.

Jennifer:	*Nikolai, where do you live?*
Дже́ннифер:	Никола́й, где вы живёте?
	[ni-kah-LAHY GD'EH-vy zhi-V'AW-ti]
Nikolai:	*I live in Russia, but I often work in America.*
Никола́й:	Я живу́ в Росси́и, но я ча́сто рабо́таю в Аме́рике.
	[ya- zhi-V'OO v-rah-SEE-i naw-yah-CHAHS-tə rah-BAW-tə-yuh vah-M'EH-ri-ki]

Jennifer: ***And where does your family live?***
Дже́ннифер: А где́ живёт ва́ша семья́?
[ah-GD^{i}EH zhi-V^{i}AWT VAH-shə sim-YAH]

Nikolai: ***My family lives in Russia.***
Никола́й: Мо́я семья́ живёт в Росси́и.
[mah-YAH sim-YAH zhi-V^{i}AWT vrah-SEE-i]

Jennifer: ***Are you alone in America?***
Дже́ннифер: Вы оди́н в Аме́рике?
[vy-ah-DEEN vah-M^{i}EH-ri-ki]

Nikolai: ***Yes, in America I live by myself.***
Никола́й: Да, я в Аме́рике живу́ оди́н.
[DAH YAH vah-M^{i}EH-ri-ki zhi-VOO ah-DEEN]

Jennifer: ***Tell me please, where do you have breakfast, lunch, and dinner?***
Дже́ннифер: Скажи́те, пожа́луйста, где вы за́втракаете, обе́даете и у́жинаете?
[skah-ZHEE-ti pah-ZHAH-ləs-tə GD^{i}EY-vy ZAHF-trə-kə-i-ti ah-B^{i}EH-də-i-ti i-OO-zhi-nə-i-ti]

Nikolai: ***I have breakfast and dinner in a café or in a restaurant.***
Никола́й: Я за́втракаю и у́жинаю в кафе́ и́ли в рестора́не.
[yah-ZAHF-trə-kə-yu i-U-zhy-nə-yu FKAH-feh i-li-vri-stah-RAH-ni]

Jennifer: ***And in Russia?***
Дже́ннифер: А в Росси́и?
[ah-vrah-SEE-i]

Nikolai: ***In Russia, I usually have breakfast and dinner at home.***
Никола́й: В Росси́и я обы́чно за́втракаю и у́жинаю до́ма.
[vrah-SEE-i yah-ah-BYCH-nə ZAHF-trə-kə-yu i-U-zhi-nə-yu DAW-mə]

Jennifer: ***And where do you have lunch in the afternoon?***
Дже́ннифер: А где вы обе́даете днём?
[ah-GD^{i}EH-vy ah-B^{i}EH-də-i-ti DN^{i}AWM]

Nikolai: ***In the afternoon, I always have lunch at work.***
Никола́й: Днём я всегда́ обе́даю на рабо́те.
[DN^{i}AWM yah-fsig-DAH ah-B^{i}EH-də-yu nə-rah-BAW-ti]

Take It Further

Notice the conjunction и́ли in Nikolai's answer: Я за́втракаю и у́жинаю в кафе́ и́ли в рестора́не. (*I have breakfast and dinner in a café or in a restaurant.*) It is equivalent to the English conjunction *or*. You should use it whenever you would use *or* in English. The only difference is that it's never preceded by a comma in Russian.

✎ Work Out 2

▶ 5G Work Out 2 (CD: 2, Track: 7)

Let's practice what you've learned.

A. Complete the sentences with one of the following time expressions—у́тром, днём, or ве́чером.

1. _У_____ я всегда́ за́втракаю до́ма.

2. _____ ты ча́сто обе́даешь в столо́вой.

3. Она́ всегда́ у́жинает до́ма _____.

4. Иногда́ мы за́втракаем _____ в кафе́.

5. Где вы обе́даете _____?

6. Где они́ у́жинают _____?

B. Complete the sentences with the appropriate form of one of the following verbs—за́втракать, обе́дать, у́жинать.

1. Утром я всегда́ _____ до́ма. (*have breakfast*)

2. Днём он обы́чно _____ на рабо́те. (*has lunch*)

3. Ве́чером мы иногда́ _____ в рестора́не. (*have dinner*)

4. Где вы _____ у́тром? (*have breakfast*)

5. Где они́ _____ днём? (*have lunch*)

6. Она́ всегда́ _____ ве́чером до́ма. (*has dinner*)

C. Now listen to the audio for more practice. This will help you master the material you've learned so far. Listen to the Russian sentences, translate them into English, and repeat them in Russian.

1. Никола́й рабо́тает на фи́рме в Аме́рике.

   _____

2. Они́ живу́т и рабо́тают в Росси́и.

   _____

3. Мы ча́сто обе́даем в столо́вой на рабо́те.

   _____

4. Где вы всегда́ за́втракаете?

   _____

5. Иногда́ я у́жинаю в рестора́не.

   _____

D. Now, listen to the English sentences, translate them into Russian, and say them out loud in Russian.

1. *I live in Russia.*

2. *He works in America.*

3. *She always has breakfast at home.*

4. *We often have lunch in a café at work.*

5. *Where do you (form. sg.) usually have lunch?*

6. *They sometimes have dinner in a restaurant.*

7. *In the morning, we have breakfast at home.*

ANSWER KEY
A. 1. Утром; 2. Днём; 3. вéчером; 4. ýтром; 5. днём; 6. вéчером
B. 1. зáвтракаю; 2. обéдает; 3. ýжинаем; 4. зáвтракаете; 5.обéдают; 6. ýжинают
C. 1. *Nikolai works at a firm in America. 2. They live and work in Russia. 3. We often have lunch in a cafeteria at work. 4. Where do you always have breakfast? 5. Sometimes, I have dinner in a restaurant.*
D. 1. Я живý в Росси́и. 2. Он рабóтает в Амéрике. 3. Онá всегдá зáвтракает дóма. 4. Мы чáсто обéдаем в кафé на рабóте. 5. Где вы обы́чно обéдаете? 6. Они́ иногдá ýжинают в рестора́не. 7. Утром мы зáвтракаем дóма.

✎ Drive It Home

The following exercise will help you master the verbs and time expressions you studied in this lesson. Write out all the answers, and read each exercise aloud.

1. Николай живёт в России, а _____ в Америке. (works)

2. Утром он всегда _____ в кафе. (has breakfast)

3. Днём они всегда _____ на работе. (have lunch)

4. Вечером мы часто _____ в ресторане. (have dinner)

5. Утром и днём я _____ в офисе на фирме. (work)

6. Они _____ и _____ в России. (live; work)

7. Вы работает в офисе или _____? (at home)

8. Где ты завтракаешь _____? (in the morning)

9. Она _____ обедает в столовой на работе? (always)

10. _____ мы ужинаем в ресторане. (sometimes)

ANSWER KEY

1. работает; 2. завтракает; 3. обедают; 4. ужинаем; 5. работаю; 6. живут, работают; 7. дома; 8. утром; 9. всегда; 10. Иногда

Parting Words

Well done! You've finished the first half of Essential Russian! By now, you should know how to:

☐ Talk about where one resides and works. (Still unsure? Go back to page 88.)

☐ Use Russian personal pronouns. (Still unsure? Go back to page 90.)

☐ Conjugate basic Russian verbs. (Still unsure? Go back to page 90.)

☐ Discuss basic daily meals. (Still unsure? Go back to page 91.)

☐ Refer to different times of day using appropriate time expressions. (Still unsure? Go back to page 93.)

☐ Put it all together in a simple conversation. (Still unsure? Go back to page 95.)

Don't forget to practice and reinforce what you've learned by visiting **www.livinglanguage.com/ languagelab** for flashcards, games, and quizzes!

Word Recall

Now let's review: change the pronouns and, consequently, the verb endings in the following sentences. Repeat them out loud.

1. Утром я за́втракаю в кафе́.

   ты _____

   он _____

   вы _____

2. Она́ рабо́тает на фи́рме в Росси́и.

   я _____

   она́ _____

   они́ _____

3. Мы ча́сто у́жинаем в рестора́не.

   вы _____

   я _____

   ты _____

4. Ты всегда́ за́втракаешь до́ма?

   мы _____

   он _____

   вы _____

Essential Russian

5. Где ты живёшь?

вы _____

они́ _____

она́ _____

Quiz 1

Контрóльная рабóта №1

kahnt-RAWL'-nə-yə rah-BAW-tə NAW-mir ah-DEEN

Now let's see how you've done so far. In this section you'll find a short quiz testing what you learned in Lessons 1–5. After you've answered all of the questions, score your quiz and see how you did! If you find that you need to go back and review, please do so before starting Lesson 6.

You'll get a second quiz after Lesson 10, followed by a final review with five dialogues and comprehension questions.

Let's get started!

A. Match the following English words to their Russian equivalents.

1. квартúра   a. *letter*

2. окнó   b. *photograph*

3. письмó   c. *apartment*

4. стол   d. *window*

5. фотогрáфия   e. *table*

B. Translate the following English expressions into Russian.

1. *Hello, Mr. Smith! Are you (form. sg.) an American?*

_____

2. *Where do you (form. sg.) live and work?*

_____

3. *Is this your (form. sg.) daughter? Is she a student?*

_____

4. *Whose things are these?*

_____

5. *These are my things.*

_____

C. Fill in the blanks with the correct form of *one.*

1. _____ де́вушка

2. _____ роди́тели

3. _____ сын

4. _____ семья

5. _____ мо́ре

D. Fill in the table with the correct personal pronouns and forms of the verbs.

I work	1.
you live (inform. sg.)	2.
she has breakfast	3.
you have lunch (pl.)	4.
we have dinner	5.

E. Complete the following sentences.

1. _____ я за́втракаю _____ . *(In the morning, in a café)*

2. Бизнесме́н рабо́тает _____ . *(in an office)*

3. Моя́ жена́ _____ . *(is at home)*

4. Я _____ обе́даю _____. *(always, at work)*

5. _____, вы журнали́стка? *(Tell me please)*

How Did You Do?

Give yourself a point for every correct answer, then use the following key to determine whether or not you're ready to move on:

0–10 points: It's probably best to go back and study the lessons again to make sure you understood everything completely. Take your time; it's not a race! Make sure you spend time reviewing the vocabulary and reading through each Grammar Builder section carefully.

11–18 points: If the questions you missed were in sections A or B, you may want to review the vocabulary from previous lessons again; if you missed answers mostly in sections C, D, or E, check the Grammar Builder sections to make sure you have your grammar basics down.

19–25 points: Feel free to move on to Lesson 6. You're doing a great job!

☐☐ **points**

Lesson 6: Talking About Where You're From

Шестóй урóк: Откýда вы?

Здрáвствуйте и ещё раз добрó пожáловать! *Hello and welcome once again!* In this sixth lesson, you'll learn how to:

☐ Say where you have been/where you were.

☐ Use the verb *to be* in the past tense.

☐ Say where you are from.

☐ Count from 1 to 4 and count things from 1 to 4.

☐ Use more time expressions and say *in the summer, fall, winter,* and *spring.*

Готóвы? (*Ready?*) Тогдá начнём! (*Then let's begin!*)

Vocabulary Builder 1

▶ 6A Vocabulary Builder 1 (CD: 2, Track: 7)

to be	быть
he was	он был
she was	она́ была́
they were	они́ бы́ли
Moscow, in Moscow	Москва́, в Москве́
New York, in New York	Нью-Йо́рк, в Нью-Йо́рке
Petersburg, in Petersburg	Петербу́рг, в Петербу́рге
Siberia, in Siberia	Сиби́рь, в Сиби́ри
when	когда́
yesterday	вчера́
in the winter	зимо́й
in the spring	весно́й
in the summer	ле́том
in the fall	о́сенью

✎ Vocabulary Practice 1

Let's practice the new vocabulary.

A. Please put the following locations in the prepositional case

1. Я живу́_____. (Москва́)

2. Она́ рабо́тает _____. (Нью-Йо́рк)

3. Ле́том мы бы́ли_____. (Петербу́рг)

4. Зимо́й они́ жи́ли_____. (Сиби́рь)

5. Когда́ она́ была́_____? (Москва́)

B. Now match the following English time expressions with their Russian
   equivalents.

   1. *in the fall*   a. ле́том
   2. *in the spring*   b. зимо́й
   3. *in the summer*   c. весно́й
   4. *in the winter*   d. о́сенью

   ANSWER KEY
   A. 1. в Москве́; 2. в Нью-Йо́рке; 3. в Петербу́рге; 4. в Сиби́ри; 5. в Москве́
   B. 1. d; 2. c; 3. a; 4. b

Grammar Builder 1
▶ 6B Grammar Builder 1 (CD: 2, Track: 9)

THE VERB БЫТЬ (*TO BE*) IN THE PAST

Although the Russian verb быть (*to be*) is left out in the present tense, you should
always use it in the past tense. The Russian past tense is very simple: for example,
быть in the past changes according to the gender and number of the subject. If
it is masculine, then the verb ends in –л; if it's feminine, the ending is –ла; if it's
neuter, it ends in –ло; and if it's plural, the ending is –ли. The –л is the past tense
marker; the following vowel (or zero) is the gender/number marker.

Consider the following paradigm:

он был	*he was (masc.)*
она́ была́	*she was (fem.)*
оно́ бы́ло	*it was (neut.)*
они́ бы́ли	*they were (pl.)*

Никола́й был в Аме́рике.
Nikolai was in America.

Дже́ннифер была́ в Москве́.
Jennifer was in Moscow.

Письмо́ бы́ло на столе́.
The letter was on the table.

Мы бы́ли в Петербу́рге.
We were in Petersburg.

Vocabulary Builder 2

▶ 6C Vocabulary Builder 2 (CD: 2, Track: 10)

where from	отку́да
from Russia	из Росси́и
from America	из Аме́рики
from Moscow	из Москвы́
from New York	из Нью-Йо́рка
from Petersburg	из Петербу́рга
two (masc. or neut.)	два
two (fem.)	две
three	три
four	четы́ре
post office	по́чта
at the post office	на по́чте
from the post office	с по́чты
store	магази́н

supermarket	суперма́ркет
market	ры́нок
at the market	на ры́нке

✎ Vocabulary Practice 2

Let's use the vocabulary you've just learned.

A. Arrange the following numerals in ascending order.

четы́ре, два, оди́н, три

_____

B. Please match the Russian phrases with their English equivalents.

1. из Петербу́рга   a. *from New York*

2. из Сиби́ри   b. *in the market*

3. с по́чты   c. *store*

4. суперма́ркет   d. *from Siberia*

5. магази́н   e. *from Petersburg*

6. на ры́нке   f. *from the post office*

7. отку́да   g. *shopping mall*

8. из Нью-Йо́рка   h. *from where*

9. из Росси́и   i. *supermarket*

10. торго́вый це́нтр   j. *from Russia*

ANSWER KEY
A. 1. оди́н; 2. два; 3. три; 4. четы́ре
B. 1. e; 2. d; 3. f; 4. i; 5. c; 6. b; 7. h; 8. a; 9. j; 10. g

Grammar Builder 2

▶ 6D Grammar Builder 2 (CD: 2, Track: 11)

THE GENITIVE CASE

Now, it's time to learn another case, the genitive case. One of the many functions of the genitive case is to indicate the place one comes from. Hence, the name of this case since *genitive* comes from *genesis*. This case has its own set of endings for masculine, feminine, and neuter nouns. Nouns in the genitive case often follow a preposition of origin, such as из or с (*from*).

For example, masculine and neuter nouns, like Петербу́рг and Нью-Йо́рк or окно́ and мо́ре, have the ending –а (or –я) in the genitive case:

Masculine	из Петербу́рга
	from Petersburg
	из Нью-Йо́рка
	from New York
Neuter	из окна́
	from/out of the window
	с мо́ря
	from the sea

Feminine nouns have the ending –ы (or –и):

Feminine	из Москвы́
	from Moscow
	из Аме́рики
	from America
	с по́чты
	from the post office

You'll learn the plural forms of the genitive case in the later lessons.

Take It Further 1

▶ 6E Take It Further 1 (CD: 2, Track: 12)

Russian nouns after the numerals 2, 3, and 4 must be in the genitive singular
(*sic*!) form. So, if you want to say *three stores*, you should say три магазина. You
should also remember that the numeral *two* changes in Russian, according to the
gender of the following noun: the form два is followed by masculine and neuter
nouns; две by feminine nouns. For example,

Masculine	два студе́нта *two students* два дома́ *two houses*
Neuter	два письма́ *two letters* два окна́ *two windows*
Feminine	две кварти́ры *two apartments* две студе́нтки *two female students*

✎ Work Out 1

A. Insert the correct past form of the verb быть (был, была́, бы́ло, бы́ли) in the
   following sentences.

1. Мой друг _____ в Аме́рике.

2. Джон_____ в Москве́. Мои́ друзья́ _____ в Нью-Йо́рке.

3. Мы то́же _____ в Нью-Йо́рке.

4. Я _____ в Петербу́рге. (female)

5. Я _____ в Москве́. (male)

B. You can use the words and expressions that you just learned to ask and say where a person was and where he, she, or they come from. As usual you'll hear the English first, then fill in the missing Russian words, and finally, repeat the correct answers in the pauses provided.

1. *Where were you yesterday?*

   Где вы_____ вчера́?

2. *Yesterday I was in the supermarket. (masc.)*

   Вчера́ я _____ в суперма́ркете.

3. *My daughter was at the post office.*

   Моя́ дочь была́_____.

4. *We were in Petersburg in the summer.*

   Мы бы́ли_____ ле́том.

5. *They were in Moscow in the fall.*

   Они́_____ в Москве́ _____.

6. *Where are you from?(inform.)*

   _____ ты?

7. *My parents are from Russia.*

   Мои́ роди́тели_____.

8. *He is an American from New York.*

   Он америка́нец_____.

9. *This is a letter from the post office.*

Это письмо́_____.

10. *Yesterday, in the morning, I was at the market. (fem.)*

Вчера́ у́тром я _____.

ANSWER KEY
A. 1. был; 2. был; 3. бы́ли; 4. бы́ли; 5. была́; 6. был
B. 1. бы́ли; 2. был; 3. на по́чте; 4. в Петербу́рге; 5. бы́ли, о́сенью; 6. Отку́да; 7. из Росси́и;
8. из Нью-Йо́рка; 9. с по́чты; 10. была́ на ры́нке

🔊 Bring It All Together
▶ 6F Bring It All Together (CD: 2, Track: 13)

Now let's listen to a dialogue that employs the structures and words from this lesson. John and Olga are talking about their native cities and their foreign travels.

Olga:	*John, where were you in the summer?*
Óльга:	Джон, где вы бы́ли ле́том?
John:	*I was in Russia.*
Джон:	Я был в Ро́ссии.
Olga:	*Where exactly?*
Óльга:	А где и́менно?
John:	*I was in Moscow and Petersburg.*
Джон:	Я был в Москве́ и в Петербу́рге.
Olga:	*How interesting! I am from Petersburg.*
Óльга:	Как интере́сно! Я из Петербу́рга.
Olga:	*This is a very beautiful city! And where are you from, John?*
Óльга:	Э́то о́чень краси́вый го́род! А вы отку́да, Джон?
John:	*I'm from New York.*
Джон:	Я из Нью-Йо́рка.
Olga:	*I've been [I was] in New York twice—in the fall and in the spring.*
Óльга:	А я была́ в Нью-Йо́рке два ра́за—о́сенью и весно́й.

| John: | New York is a very interesting city. |
| Джон: | Нью-Йо́рк—о́чень интере́сный го́род. |

Take It Further 2

▶ 6G Take It Further 2 (CD: 2, Track: 14)

The Russian word for *time* (when you count the times you've done something) is
раз. It's masculine, so it will be modified by the numerals 1 to 4 in the following
way:

оди́н раз
one time, once

два ра́за
two times, twice

три ра́за
three times

четы́ре ра́за
four times

Ско́лько раз asks *how many times*. The quantifier ско́лько requires the genitive
plural form, but the word раз is exceptional—its genitive plural coincides with
the nominative singular.

✎ Work Out 2
▶ 6H Work Out 2 (CD: 2, Track 15)

A. It's time to practice. First, complete the sentences with the correct preposition and case; follow the logic of the sentence when you decide between the prepositional case (stationary location) and the genitive case (one's origin). Then, repeat the full sentence out loud. Imagine a situation when you'd say it.

1. Джон – америка́нец. Он _____ Нью-Йо́рк____.

2. Джон был ле́том в Росси́и. Он был ____ Петербу́рг____.

3. Ско́лько раз вы бы́ли ____ Аме́рик____?

4. Вчера́ ве́чером я был ____ магази́н____.

5. Вы ру́сская? Да, я _____ Росси́____.

6. Где они́ живу́т? Они́ живу́т ____ Росси́____.

7. Ле́том мы бы́ли ____ Москв____.

8. Утром они́ бы́ли _____ ры́нк____.

9. Мои́ друзья́ – ру́сские. Они́ _____ Москв____.

10. Днём я была́ _____ по́чт____.

B. Listen to the Russian sentences, translate them into English, and then repeat them in Russian.

1. Я была́ два ра́за в Аме́рике.

_____

2. Ле́том я был в Росси́и.

_____

3. Вы из Росси́и? Из Петербу́рга?

_____

4. Вчера́ ве́чером мы бы́ли в магази́не.

_____

5. Зимо́й они́ бы́ли в Нью-Йо́рке.

_____

C. Now, listen to the English sentences, translate them into Russian, and say them out loud in Russian.

1. *Where were you in the summer? (inform. fem.)*

_____

2. *Where are you from? (form.)*

_____

3. *They are from Petersburg.*

_____

4. *This is a letter from the post office.*

_____

5. *In the morning, she was in the store.*

_____

ANSWER KEY

A. 1. из, –а; 2. в, –е; 3. в, –е; 4. в, –е; 5. из, –и; 6. в, –и; 7. в, –е; 8. на, –е; 9. из, –ы; 10. на, –е
B. 1. *I've been to America twice. 2. I was in Russia in the summer. 3. Are you from Russia? From Petersburg? 4. Last night, we were at the store. 5. In the winter, they were in New York.*
C. 1. Где ты была́ ле́том? 2. Отку́да вы? 3. Они́ из Петербу́рга. 4. Э́то письмо́ с по́чты.
5. Утром она́ была́ в магази́не.

✎ Drive It Home

Now, it's time to drive home the main grammatical points of the lesson.

A. Count the following people and things in Russian.

1. *one time* _____

2. *two times* _____

3. *three times* _____

4. *four times* _____

5. *one [female] student* _____

6. *two [female] students* _____

7. *one businessman* _____

8. *two businessmen* _____

B. Insert the correct form of the verb *to be* in the past tense.

Кто где был? (*Who was where?*)

1. Америка́нский бизнесме́н _____ в Москве́.

2. Мой муж _____ в Москве́.

3. Моя́ жена́ _____ в Петербу́рге.

4. Моя́ студе́нка _____ в Петербу́рге.

5. На́ши де́ти _____ в Росси́и.

6. Мои́ студе́нты _____ в Росси́и.

7. Мои́ роди́тели _____ в Росси́и.

ANSWER KEY
A. 1. оди́н раз; 2. два ра́за; 3. три ра́за; 4. четы́ре ра́за; 5. одна́ студе́нтка; 6. две студе́нтки;
7. один бизнесме́н; 8. два бизнесме́на
B. 1. был; 2. был; 3. была́; 4. была́; 5. бы́ли; 6. бы́ли; 7. бы́ли

Take It Further 3

All Russian endings fall under two general categories: hard and soft. Hard endings
follow hard consonants and soft endings follow soft consonants to maintain vowel
correspondence.

VOWELS IN HARD ENDINGS	VOWELS IN SOFT ENDINGS
а	я
о	ё
у	ю
ы	и
э	е

However, an additional complication interferes with this fairly straightforward
system and overrides it. This complication is usually referred to as the spelling
rule. The spelling rule concerns only eight consonants: four hushers (because
they produce a hushing sound)—ж, ш, щ, ч; three gutturals (because they are
pronounced in the back of your mouth)—г, к, х; and the letter ц. Here's the rule:

All gutturals and all hushers must be followed by the letters: а, у, and и (and
never by я, ю, ы). All hushers and ц must be followed by either a stressed о or an
unstressed е. The letter ц can be followed by an ы in the end of the word and by
an и in the middle.

Memorize this spelling rule and always keep it in mind along with the above
chart! They will take the mystery out of the Russian endings and will dramatically
reduce what you otherwise would have to memorize mechanically.

Parting Words

Congratulations on finishing six lessons! In this lesson, you learned how to:

☐ Say where you have been/where you were. (Still unsure? Go back to page 108.)

☐ Use more time expressions and say in the summer, fall, winter, and spring. (Still unsure? Go back to page 108.)

☐ Use the verb *to be* in the past tense. (Still unsure? Go back to page 109.)

☐ Say where you are from. (Still unsure? Go back to page 110.)

☐ Count from 1 to 4 and count things from 1 to 4. (Still unsure? Go back to page 113.)

Don't forget to practice and reinforce what you've learned by visiting **www.livinglanguage.com/ languagelab** for flashcards, games, and quizzes!

Word Recall

Time to review the vocabulary from the previous six lessons. Choose the word that fits best in the blanks.

в ко́мнате, в кафе́, у́тром, рабо́тает, семья́, три ра́за, мои́ ве́щи, де́ти, скажи́те, пожа́луйста, у́жинаем

1. _____, отку́да вы?

2. Я и мой муж из Росси́и. На́ши _____ хорошо́ говоря́т по-ру́сски. Это письмо́ бы́ло на столе́ _____.

3. Ве́чером мы всегда́ _____ до́ма.

4. На фотогра́фии моя́ _____.

5. Мы бы́ли в Аме́рике _____.

6. Я ча́сто за́втракаю _____.

7. Они́ бы́ли на ры́нке _____.

8. _____ бы́ли в шкафу́.

9. Он бизнесме́н и _____ в о́фисе.

ANSWER KEY
1. Скажи́те, пожа́луйста; 2. де́ти; 3. в ко́мнате; 4. у́жинаем; 5. семья́; 6. три ра́за; 7. в кафе́; 8. у́тром; 9. Мои́ ве́щи; 10. рабо́тает

Essential Russian

Lesson 7: At a Restaurant

Седьмо́й уро́к: В рестора́не

Добро́ пожа́ловать в седьмо́й уро́к! *Welcome to Lesson 7!* In this lesson, you'll learn how to:

☐ Talk about eating and drinking.

☐ Use the accusative case.

☐ Talk about your food preferences.

☐ Use the future tense.

☐ Use the verbs in the past tense.

Гото́вы продолжа́ть? Тогда́ начнём! *Ready to continue? Then, let's begin!* Let's get started with some new words and phrases.

Vocabulary Builder 1

▶ 7A Vocabulary Builder 1 (CD: 2, Track: 16)

to speak	говори́ть
to like	люби́ть
what, that	что
for breakfast	на за́втрак
for lunch	на обе́д
for dinner	на у́жин
for/as appetizer	на заку́ску
for dessert	на десе́рт
soup	суп
chicken	ку́рица
salad	сала́т
bread	хлеб
coffee	ко́фе
tea	чай
milk	молоко́

✎ Vocabulary Practice 1

Can you fill in the missing Russian or English words in the pairs below? Repeat the Russian word out loud. Make sure you remember its spelling.

breakfast	*1.*
2.	ко́фе
3.	говори́ть
dinner	*4.*
5.	молоко́
salad	*6.*

to like	*7.*
8.	ку́рица
9.	меню́
tea	*10.*
11.	десе́рт
12.	обе́д
bread	*13.*
14.	суп

ANSWER KEY

1. за́втрак; 2. *coffee*; 3. *to speak*; 4. ужин; 5. *milk*; 6. сала́т; 7. люби́ть; 8. *chicken*; 9. *menu*; 10. чай;
11. *dessert*; 12. *lunch*; 13. хлеб; 14. *soup*

Grammar Builder 1

▶ 7B Grammar Builder 1 (CD: 2, Track: 17)

THE ACCUSATIVE CASE

The verbs люби́ть (*to like*) and говори́ть (*to speak*) belong to Type II of the
conjugation types. As you learned in Lesson 5, Type II is very close to Type I
except that the verbs of this type have an –и in their endings (instead of an –е
in Type I) and have the endings –ат/–ят in the они́ form (instead of –ут/–ют in
Type I). Take a look at the following paradigm:

SINGULAR	PLURAL
я люблю́ *I like*	мы лю́бим *we like*
ты лю́бишь *you like*	вы лю́бите *you like*
он/она́ лю́бит *he/she likes*	они́ лю́бят *they like*

Notice two peculiarities in this verb's conjugation: 1. the first person singular form has an additional letter л—the so-called л–mutation and 2. the stress shifts from the first person singular ending back to the stem of the verb. These peculiarities—mutation and stress shift—will reoccur in many other Russian verbs. This stress pattern is found in many present tense verbs of both types. The mutation patterns will vary and we'll comment on them in later lessons. Recognizing these peculiarities when you study new verbs will make learning them easier.

Now it's time to learn one more case—the accusative. The direct object of the verb любить (to like) is the object of liking, e.g., мясо, рыба, чай, etc. Direct objects in Russian must be in the accusative case.

The accusative case is easy: all masculine and neuter singular nouns and all plural nouns stay the same; all feminine nouns ending in an –a have the ending –y. (However, be aware of one important exception: masculine singular nouns denoting people and animals, i.e., animate nouns, and all plural animate nouns use the genitive case ending instead of the accusative; we will discuss this exception in later lessons.) So far, with the exception of masculine singular and all plural animate nouns, you need to worry only about nouns ending in an –a. And here's your rule of thumb: in the accusative case, all –a endings become –y endings. For example:

masc. sg. inanimate noun—no change	Я люблю́ хлеб. I like bread.
neut. sg. inanimate noun—no change	Я люблю́ молоко́. I like milk.
fem. sg. noun—the –a ending becomes –y	Я люблю́ ку́рицу. I like chicken.
plural inanimate noun—no change	Я люблю́ о́вощи. I like vegetables.

Vocabulary Builder 2

▶ 7C Vocabulary Builder 2 (CD: 2, Track: 18)

to want	хотéть
water (nom. case), water (acc. case)	водá, вóду
orange juice	апельсúновый сок
apple juice	я́блочный сок
meat	мя́со
fish	ры́ба
what side dish	какóй гарнúр
potatoes	картóфель (*sg. only*), картóшка (*sg. only, coll.*)
pasta (lit., macaroni)	макарóны (*pl. only*), пáста
rice	рис
cheese	сыр
fruit	фрýкты
ice cream	морóженое
(Would you) pass (me the) salt, please.	Передáйте, пожáлуйста, соль.
pepper	пéрец
sugar	сáхар
What will you have?/What would you like?	Что вы бýдете?
I'll have fish.	Я бýду ры́бу.

✎ Vocabulary Practice 2

Now let's practice. Match the English expressions in the left column with their Russian equivalents on the right.

1. *fruits*   a. я́блочный сок

2. *(Would you) pass (me) salt, please.*   b. Что вы бу́дете?

3. *orange juice*   c. вода́

4. *cheese*   d. Переда́йте, пожа́луйста, соль.

5. *I'll have fish.*   e. апельси́новый сок

6. *meat*   f. макаро́ны, па́ста

7. *pasta*   g. фру́кты

8. *What will you have?*   h. сыр

9. *apple juice*   i. Я бу́ду ры́бу.

10. *water*   j. мя́со

ANSWER KEY
1. g; 2. d; 3. e; 4. h; 5. i; 6. j; 7. f; 8. b; 9. a; 10. c

Grammar Builder 2

▶ 7D Grammar Builder 2 (CD: 2, Track: 19)

THE VERBS БУ́ДУ **(WILL) AND** ХОТЕ́ТЬ **(TO WANT)**

The Russian sentence, Я бу́ду ры́бу (*I will have fish*), translates literally as *I will … fish*. The omitted verb—either *eat*, *have*, or *order*—is implied. The verb, бу́ду, is an auxiliary verb *will* which expresses the future tense. This is a Type I verb and its conjugation is as follows.

SINGULAR	PLURAL
я бу́ду	мы бу́дем
I will	*we will*

SINGULAR	PLURAL
ты бу́дешь	вы бу́дете
you will	*you will*
он, она́ бу́дет	они́ бу́дут
he/she will	*they will*

Together with the following infinitive, this verb forms the future tense. For example:

Я бу́ду говори́ть по-ру́сски.
I will speak Russian.

Мы бу́дем говори́ть по-ру́сски.
We will speak Russian., etc.

The conjugation of the verb хоте́ть (*to want*) is irregular because it blends Type I in the singular with Type II in the plural. Take a look at the following paradigm:

SINGULAR	PLURAL
я хочу́	мы хоти́м
I want	*we want*
ты хо́чешь	вы хоти́те
you want	*you want*
он, она́ хо́чет	они́ хотя́т
he, she wants	*they want*

Notice the stress shift in the singular forms from the ending back to the stem (the stress in the plural form is stable). Notice also the т/ч mutation in the singular (but not in the plural).

Take It Further 1

▶ 7E take It Further 1 (CD: 2, Track: 20)

There are some patterns to irregularities such as mutations and stress shifts, which will help you learn them.

Remember that if stress shifts in the present tense, it shifts only from the first-person singular ending back to the stem in all of its other forms:

я	люблю́	I love, like
ты	лю́бишь	you love, like
он, она́	лю́бит	he, she loves, likes
мы	лю́бим	we love, like
вы	лю́бите	you love, like
они́	лю́бят	they love, like

However, if stress shifts in the past, it follows two similar patterns: 1) it "goes out" for the feminine ending and stays on the stem in all other forms. For example,

он	был	he was
она́	была́	she was
оно́	бы́ло	it was
они́	бы́ли	they were

2) In some past tense verbs, which we will talk about in later chapters, stress stays on the stem only in the masculine form but shifts to the end in all other forms. This type of stress pattern is called "end stress." For example, consider the past tense of the Russian verb to bring, принести́:

он	принёс	he brought
она́	принесла́	she brought
оно́	принесло́	it brought

они́	принесли́	*they brought*

If a mutation occurs in a Type I verb, it occurs throughout all six forms. In Type II verbs, it occurs only in the first-person singular form. For example,

TYPE I	TYPE II
ПИСа́ТЬ (*TO WRITE*) [С/Ш-MUTATION]	ЛЮБи́ТЬ (*TO LIKE, TO LOVE*) [Л-MUTATION]
я пишу́	я люблю́
ты пи́шешь	ты лю́бишь
он, она́ пи́шет	он, она́ лю́бит
мы пи́шем	мы лю́бим
вы пи́шете	вы лю́бите
они́ пи́шут	они́ лю́бят

And finally, stress shifts and mutations, if they occur at all, occur either in the past tense or in the present, but never in both tenses simultaneously.

✎ Work Out 1

Now, let's practice what you've just learned.

A. Tell the waiter what you'd like to order. Use the construction я бу́ду + Acc. Remember to put the things you'd like to have into the accusative case!
Что вы бу́дете?

1. Я бу́ду _____. (*cheese*)

2. Я бу́ду _____. (*meat*)

3. Я бу́ду _____. (*fish*)

4. Я бу́ду _____. (apple juice)

5. Я бу́ду _____. (salad)

6. Я бу́ду _____. (chicken)

7. Я бу́ду _____. (tea)

8. Я бу́ду _____. (fruits)

9. Я бу́ду _____. (water)

10. Я бу́ду _____. (pasta)

B. Fill in the blanks with the appropriate forms of the verbs люби́ть (to like), хоте́ть (to want, would like), and быть (to be—in the future form).

1. Я _____ апельси́новый сок на за́втрак. (want)

2. Что ты _____ на обе́д? (will [have])

3. Мы _____ ку́рицу и рис на у́жин. (want)

4. Вы _____ ры́бу? (like)

5. Она́ о́чень _____ фру́кты и о́вощи на обе́д. (want)

6. Он _____ сала́т на заку́ску. (will [have])

7. Мы _____ у́жинать в рестора́не. (will)

8. Какой гарни́р ты _____, карто́фель, рис и́ли па́сту? (want)

9. На десе́рт я _____ моро́женое. (will [have])

10. Я не хочу́ вино́, я _____ про́сто во́ду. (will [have])

ANSWER KEY

A. 1. сыр; 2. мя́со; 3. ры́бу; 4. я́блочный сок; 5. сала́т; 6. ку́рицу; 7. чай; 8. фру́кты; 9. во́ду;
10. па́сту
B. 1. хочу́; 2. бу́дешь; 3. хоти́м; 4. лю́бите; 5. хо́чет; 6. бу́дет; 7. бу́дем; 8. хо́чешь; 9. бу́ду; 10. бу́ду

🔊 Bring It All Together

▶ 7F Bring It All Together (CD: 2, Track: 21)

Listen to the following conversation in a restaurant that highlights the structures you have learned in this lesson and introduces a bit more vocabulary. A Russian waiter, Vladimir, is speaking with an American customer, Jane.

Jane:	*Hello.*
Джейн:	Здра́вствуйте.
Vladimir:	*Hi and welcome! Here is our menu. Would you like [Will you have] anything to drink?*
Влади́мир:	Здра́вствуйте и добро́ пожа́ловать! Пожа́луйста, вот на́ше меню́. Вы бу́дете что́-нибудь пить?
Jane:	*Water, please.*
Джейн:	Во́ду, пожа́луйста.
Vladimir:	*One minute.*
Влади́мир:	Одну́ мину́ту.

One minute later.
Че́рез мину́ту.

Vladimir:	*Here you go, here's your water. Have you decided what you'd like?*
Влади́мир:	Пожа́луйста, вот ва́ша вода́. Вы уже́ реши́ли, что вы бу́дете?
Jane:	*Yes, as an appetizer, I'll have salad, then soup and fish.*
Джейн:	Да, на заку́ску я бу́ду сала́т, пото́м суп и ры́бу.
Vladimir:	*And what side dish would you like, potatoes or rice?*
Влади́мир:	А како́й гарни́р вы хоти́те, карто́фель и́ли рис?

Jane:	I'll have potatoes.
Джейн:	Я буду́ карто́фель.
Vladimir:	Would you like (lit., And will you have) bread?
Влади́мир:	А хлеб бу́дете?
Jane:	Yes, please.
Джейн:	Да, пожа́луйста.
Vladimir:	Would you like (lit., Will you have) anything for dessert?
Влади́мир:	Бу́дете что́-нибу́дь на десе́рт?
Jane:	No, thank you, just tea and sugar.
Джейн:	Нет, спаси́бо, то́лько чай и са́хар.
Vladimir:	Very well. Thank you for (your) order.
Влади́мир:	О́чень хорошо́. Спаси́бо за зака́з.

Take It Further 2

▶ 7G Take It Further 2 (CD: 2, Track: 22)

Now, let's learn two essential Russian verbs—*to eat* and *to drink*.

Since the verb *to eat* has for centuries been used quite frequently, it has resisted many linguistic changes in its most common, singular forms. These were the changes that other verbs have gone through over the years. Therefore, this verb has preserved ancient features in the singular and now it appears to be irregular.

ЕСТЬ TO EAT	
PRESENT SINGULAR (IRREGULAR)	**PRESENT PLURAL (TYPE II)**
я ем	мы еди́м
I eat	*we eat*
ты ешь	вы еди́те
you eat	*you eat*
он, она́ ест	они́ едя́т
he/she eats	*they eat*

PAST
он ел *he ate*
она́ е́ла *she ate*
они́ е́ли *they ate*

пить *TO DRINK* **(TYPE I)**	
SINGULAR	**PLURAL**
я пью *I drink*	мы пьём *we drink*
ты пьёшь *you drink*	вы пьёте *you drink*
он, она́ пьёт *he/she drinks*	они́ пьют *they drink*

PAST (STRESS SHIFT)
он пил *he drank*
она́ пила́ *she drank*
они́ пи́ли *they drank*

As you can see, the above patterns are only partially irregular: generally they follow the standard paradigms for first (пить, *to drink*) and second (есть, *to eat*) conjugations.

✎ Work Out 2

▶ 7H Work Out 2 (CD: 2, Track: 23)

A. Decide whether these people had the following items for breakfast, or lunch, or dinner. Make the most logical choice.

1. Я éла суп и салáт _____.

2. Мы пи́ли ко́фе _____.

3. Мы éли мя́со и картóфель _____.

4. Он пил апельси́новый сок _____.

5. Они́ éли макарóны и пи́ли винó _____.

B. Say what you usually (обы́чно) have for breakfast, lunch, dinner, dessert, and as an appetizer. Choose from the given list of items but remember to put them in the accusative case!

1. На зáвтрак я обы́чно пью _____. (винó, чай, пи́во)

2. На обéд я обы́чно ем _____. (макарóны, суп, мя́со)

3. На у́жин я обы́чно ем _____. (фру́кты, морóженое, ку́рица и рис)

4. На десéрт я обы́чно ем _____. (ры́ба, хлеб, морóженое)

5. На закýску я обы́чно ем _____. (салáт, картóфель, рис)

C. Listen to the Russian sentences and give the English equivalents.

1. Передáйте, пожáлуйста, соль!

2. Что вы бу́дете на заку́ску?

_____

3. Что вы бу́дете на десе́рт?

_____

4. На за́втрак я пью апельси́новый сок.

_____

5. Я люблю́ ры́бу.

_____

D. Now, give Russian equivalents to the English sentences you'll hear.

1. _I like pasta._

_____

2. _Do you (form.) like cheese?_

_____

3. _I'll have soup and salad for lunch._

_____

4. _They will have fruit for breakfast._

_____

5. _We like coffee and milk._

_____

ANSWER KEY
A. 1. на обе́д; 2. на за́втрак; 3. на у́жин; 4. на за́втрак; 5. на у́жин
B. 1. чай; 2. суп; 3. ку́рицу и рис; 4. моро́женое; 5. сала́т
C. 1. _Pass the salt, please!_ 2. _What will you have for an appetizer?_ 3. _What will you have for dessert?_
4. _For breakfast, I drink orange juice._ 5. _I like fish._

D. 1. Я люблю́ па́сту. 2. Вы лю́бите сыр? 3. Я бу́ду суп и сала́т на обе́д. 4. Они́ бу́дут фру́кты на за́втрак. 5. Мы лю́бим ко́фе и молоко́.

✎ Drive It Home

Let's practice the grammar points of the lesson and try to make some of the structures you've learned a bit more automatic. Remember to write down the exercises, and read them out loud as well.

A. Fill in the blanks with the correct form of the verb in parentheses.

1. Что вы _____ на за́втрак? (like)

2. Я _____ пить ко́фе на за́втрак. (will)

3. Вы _____ по-ру́сски? (speak)

4. Ты _____ о́вощи? (like)

5. Что они́ _____ на обе́д? (will [have])

6. Он _____ моро́женое на десе́рт. (will [have])

B. Fill in the blanks with the correct noun in the accusative case.

1. Вчера́ мы е́ли _____ на у́жин. (fish)

2. Вчера́ мы е́ли _____ на у́жин. (bread)

3. Я бу́ду _____ и _____. (vegetables, fruit)

4. Мы бу́дем пить про́сто _____. (water)

5. Он всегда́ пьёт _____ на за́втрак. (milk)

6. Она́ всегда́ ест _____ на десе́рт. (ice cream)

ANSWER KEY
A. 1. лю́бите; 2. бу́ду; 3. говори́те; 4. лю́бишь; 5. бу́дут; 6. бу́дет
B. 1. ры́бу; 2. хлеб; 3. о́вощи, фру́кты; 4. во́ду; 5. молоко́; 6. моро́женое

Take It Further 3

▶ 7I Take It Further 3 (CD: 2, Track: 24)

Here are a few more expression related to eating and drinking that you may want to learn:

Enjoy your meal! Bon appétit!	Прия́тного аппети́та!
You're welcome! (only in response to "thank you" for food or drinks)	На здоро́вье!
To (everyone's) health! (a toast)	За здоро́вье!
To your health! (a toast)	Ва́ше здоро́вье!
(May I/we have the) check please!	Счёт, пожа́луйста!

Parting Words

In this lesson, you learned how to:

☐ Talk about eating and drinking. (Still unsure? Go back to page 124.)

☐ Use the accusative case. (Still unsure? Go back to page 125.)

☐ Talk about your food preferences. (Still unsure? Go back to page 127.)

☐ Use the future tense. (Still unsure? Go back to page 129.)

☐ Use the verbs in the past tense. (Still unsure? Go back to page 130.)

Don't forget to practice and reinforce what you've learned by visiting **www.livinglanguage.com/languagelab** for flashcards, games, and quizzes!

Word Recall

Let's go over some of the important vocabulary from all previous lessons. Fill in the blanks with the Russian words from the word bank below that best fit the story line.

ле́том, ве́чером, бы́ли, живу́т, друзья́, по-ру́сски, из Росси́и, в Росси́и

Вчера́ _____ мы _____ в рестора́не в Нью-Йо́рке. Там тоже бы́ли на́ши ру́сские _____. Они́ журнали́сты. Мы мно́го говори́ли _____. Они́ _____ и рабо́тают в Аме́рике, но они́ _____, из Москвы́. _____ я и моя́ жена́ бы́ли ____ _____.

Lesson 8: Countries and Languages

Восьмо́й уро́к: Стра́ны и языки́

Как всегда́, мы ра́ды вас ви́деть! *As always, we're glad to see you!* In this lesson, you'll learn how to:

☐ Speak about different countries.

☐ Speak about different nationalities and languages.

☐ Differentiate between going to a place and being there.

☐ Use the accusative case of direction.

☐ Use adjectives in the nominative case.

Гото́вы? Тогда́ начнём! *Ready? Then, let's begin!*
Let's get started with some new words and phrases.

Vocabulary Builder 1

▶ 8A Vocabulary Builder 1 (CD: 2, Track: 25)

Russia	Росси́я
The United States of America, USA	Соединённые Шта́ты Аме́рики, США
France, in France	Фра́нция, во Фра́нции
Italy	Ита́лия
Germany	Герма́ния
China	Кита́й
Japan	Япо́ния
Argentina	Аргенти́на
Egypt	Еги́пет
to rest, to vacation	отдыха́ть
Where to?	куда́?
Where did he go to? (vehicular, non-local movement)	Куда́ он е́здил?
Where did he go to? (local movement on foot or otherwise)	Куда́ он ходи́л?
Where was he?	Где он был?

✎ Vocabulary Practice 1

Let's see what countries you know. Match the English words on the left with the correct Russian name of the country on the right.

1. *Italy*   a. Еги́пет

2. *France*   b. Япо́ния

3. *Argentina*   c. Соединённые Шта́ты Аме́рики

4. *China*   d. Ита́лия

5. *Egypt*

6. *Russia*

7. *The United States of America*

8. *Japan*

e. Аргенти́на

f. Фра́нция

g. Кита́й

h. Росси́я

ANSWER KEY

1. d; 2. f; 3. e; 4. g; 5. a; 6. h; 7. c; 8. b

Grammar Builder 1

▶ 8B Grammar Builder 1 (CD: 2, Track: 26)

TALKING ABOUT GOING TO AND BEING SOMEWHERE

The English verb *to go* has many equivalents in Russian, specific to various forms of motion. We will cover some of the basic verbs of motion in later chapters. For now, however, remember that the Russian verb ходи́ть in the past tense—and in the past tense only—refers exclusively to a non-vehicular, local movement that was already completed and the person who completed it is already back at his or her original location. The verb е́здить in the past tense refers to the same type of completed movement except that the person who is back now, traveled by any kind of vehicle—a car, bus, train, horse, etc. Both verbs take the accusative case of direction, which indicates the place one walked or traveled to. Compare the following examples. Local movements (on foot or otherwise): Он ходи́л в рестора́н means that *he went to a restaurant and now he's back at home*; it's a local activity and it's irrelevant as to whether he walked there or took a cab or the metro. Она́ ходи́ла в магази́н means that *she went to a store and now she's back at home*. Они́ ходи́ли на по́чту means that *they went to a local post office and now they are back at home*.

vs.

Vehicular travels to other geographical locations: Он е́здил в Росси́ю means that *he went to Russia and now he's back*. Она́ е́здила в Аргенти́ну means that *she*

went to Argentina and now she's back.
Они́ е́здили в Москву́ means that *they went to Moscow and now they are back.*

On the other hand, the Russian verb *to be* is a stative, not a motion, verb. It takes the prepositional case of location (as opposed to the accusative of direction above). So you need to say,

Он был в рестора́не.
He was in a restaurant.

Она́ была́ в Росси́и.
She was in Russia.

Они́ бы́ли в Москве́.
They were in Moscow.

Take It Further 1
▶ 8C Take It Further 1 (CD: 2, Track: 27)

In the present tense, the verbs ходи́ть and е́здить refer to recurrent or habitual actions or actions in general. Ходи́ть refers to a non-vehicular or local movement; е́здить refers to a vehicular/non-local movement. This is how they conjugate:

я хожу́	*I go*
ты хо́дишь	*you go*
он, она́ хо́дит	*he/she goes*
мы хо́дим	*we go*
вы хо́дите	*you go*
они́ хо́дят	*they go*

This is a Type II verb. Notice the change from д to ж in the я form and the typical present tense stress shift from the ending in the я form back to the stem.

я е́зжу	I go
ты е́здишь	you go
он, она́ е́здит	he/she goes
мы е́здим	we go
вы е́здите	you go
они́ е́здят	they go

This is also a Type II verb. Once again, notice the change from д to ж in the я form and the stable stress. Consider the following examples:

Утром я хожу́ на рабо́ту.

In the morning, I go to work. (a local movement on foot or otherwise)

Ле́том мы всегда́ е́здим в Росси́ю.

In the summer, we always go to Russia. (a vehicular movement to another geographical place)

Мы ча́сто хо́дим в рестора́н.

We often go to a restaurant. (a local activity on foot or otherwise)

Vocabulary Builder 2
▶ 8D Vocabulary Builder 2 (CD: 2, Track: 28)

country	страна́
state (not a sovereign country)	штат
beautiful	краси́вый

big	большо́й
small	ма́ленький
interesting	интере́сный
old	ста́рый
new	но́вый
to speak Russian	говори́ть по-ру́сски
to speak English	говори́ть по-англи́йски
to speak French	говори́ть по-францу́зски
to speak German	говори́ть по-неме́цки
to speak Chinese	говори́ть по-кита́йски
to speak Japanese	говори́ть по-япо́нски
to speak Spanish	говори́ть по-испа́нски
to speak Arabic	говори́ть по-ара́бски

✎ Vocabulary Practice 2

Match the following countries in the left column to the languages spoken there.

1. В Росси́и говоря́т   a. по-неме́цки

2. В Аме́рике говоря́т   b. по-япо́нски

3. В Аргенти́не говоря́т   c. по-ара́бски

4. В Еги́пте говоря́т   d. по-ру́сски

5. В Герма́нии говоря́т   e. по-фра́нцузски

6. В Ита́лии говоря́т   f. по-испа́нски

7. Во Фра́нции говоря́т   g. по-италья́нски

8. В Япо́нии говоря́т   h. по-англи́йски

ANSWER KEY
1. d; 2. h; 3. f; 4. c; 5. a; 6. g; 7. e; 8. b

Grammar Builder 2

▶ 8E Grammar Builder 2 (CD: 2, Track: 29)

ADJECTIVES IN THE NOMINATIVE CASE

The expressions по-ру́сски, по-англи́йски, etc. are adverbs. They modify the manner in which one speaks and can literally be translated as *"in the Russian manner"* or *"Russianly"*, *"in the English manner"*, or *"Englishly"*, etc. Careful! All adverbs or adjectives derived from nations or countries aren't capitalized in Russian.

Also notice the lack of subject in the sentence: В Росси́и говоря́т по-ру́сски. (*In Russia [they] speak Russian.*) Remember to put the verb into the они́ form (third-person plural—not singular!) in this type of subjectless sentence.

The words краси́вый, большо́й, ма́ленький, интере́сный, ста́рый, но́вый are adjectives. In dictionaries, all Russian adjectives are listed in the nominative singular form. However, in speech they take the number, gender, and case of the noun they modify. Although Russian adjectives "agree" with the nouns they modify, their endings are slightly different from the corresponding noun endings. As a rule, Russian adjectives have either two or three letters for an ending (as opposed to nouns, which have just one letter for an ending). This is how you should make adjectives agree with nouns in the nominative case:

MASCULINE SG.	FEMININE SG.	NEUTER SG.	PLURAL
но́вый го́род	но́вая страна́	но́вое окно́	но́вые ве́щи
большо́й го́род	больша́я страна́	большо́е окно́	больши́е ве́щи

Notice that when the masculine singular ending is stressed, it's –ой, not –ый.

✎ Work Out 1

▶ 8F Work Out 1 (CD: 2, Track: 30)

Now let's review what you've just learned about adjectives. You'll hear brief statements about different countries and cities. You'll hear adjectives and nouns together in the nominative case. You'll hear the English first, then the Russian. You'll have to fill in the adjectives in their correct form, then listen to the Russian again, and repeat the entire statement for practice.

1. *Russia is an interesting country.*

   Росси́я – _____ страна́.

2. *Japan is a small country.*

   Япо́ния – _____ страна́.

3. *France is an old country.*

   Фра́нция – _____ страна́.

4. *Moscow is an old city.*

   Москва́ – _____ го́род.

5. *New York is a very interesting city.*

   Нью-Йорк – о́чень _____ го́род.

6. *Texas is a big state.*

   Теха́с – _____ штат.

7. *Connecticut is a small state.*

   Конне́ктикут – _____ штат.

8. *America and Russia are beautiful countries.*

   Аме́рика и Росси́я – _____ стра́ны.

9. *Hawaii is a new state.*

    Гава́йи – _____ штат.

10. *St. Petersburg is a beautiful city.*

    Санкт-Петербу́рг – _____ го́род.

    ANSWER KEY
    1. интере́сная; 2. ма́ленькая; 3. ста́рая; 4. ста́рый; 5. интере́сный; 6. большо́й; 7. ма́ленький;
    8. краси́вые; 9. но́вый; 10. краси́вый

✎ Bring It All Together
▶ 8G Bring It All Together (CD: 2, Track: 31)

Now let's listen to a dialogue that highlights the structures and words from this lesson. Bill and Sveta are discussing their foreign travels.

Sveta:	*Bill, have you been to Russia?*
Све́та:	Билл, вы бы́ли в Росси́и?
Bill:	*Yes, I went to Russia in the summer.*
Билл:	Да, я е́здил в Росси́ю ле́том.
Sveta:	*And where were you in Russia?*
Све́та:	А где вы бы́ли в Росси́и?
Bill:	*I was in Moscow. I also went to St. Petersburg and Novgorod.*
Билл:	Я был в Москве́. Я ещё е́здил в Санкт-Петербу́рг и в Но́вгород.
Sveta:	*Those are beautiful Russian cities.*
Све́та:	Э́то краси́вые ру́сские города́.
Bill:	*Yes, they are very interesting and Novgorod is so old!*
Билл:	Да, они́ о́чень интере́сные, а Но́вгород тако́й ста́рый!
Sveta:	*Did you speak Russian there?*
Све́та:	Вы там говори́ли по-ру́сски?
Bill:	*Of course! I always speak Russian in Russia.*
Билл:	Коне́чно! Я всегда́ говорю́ по-ру́сски в Росси́и.

Take It Further 2

▶ 8H Take It Further 2 (CD: 2, Track: 32)

Notice two "intensifiers" in the dialogue—о́чень and тако́й. О́чень means *very*; it's an adverb and it never changes; it normally precedes the adjective it intensifies. However, unlike the English *so* or *such*, тако́й is an adjective; therefore, it has the same ending as the adjective it intensifies:

Москва́ – тако́й большо́й го́род.
Moscow is such a big city.

Но́вгород тако́й ста́рый.
Novgorod is so old.

Росси́я – така́я больша́я страна́.
Russia is such a big country.

On the other hand, when *so* in Russian intensifies adverbs—not adjectives—it assumes an adverbial, uninflected form так. For example, you should say:

Она́ так хорошо́ говори́т по-ру́сски.
She speaks Russian so well.

✎ Work Out 2

▶ 8l Work Out 2 (CD: 2, Track 33)

A. Say where these people went. Remember to use the correct form of the verb *to go*: ходи́ть—for a local non-vehicular motion and е́здить—for non-local, vehicular motion.

1. Ле́том я_____ в Росси́ю. (*went; masc.*)

2. Зимо́й мы_____ в Ита́лию. (*went*)

3. Утром они́ _____на рабо́ту. (*went*)

4. Днём вы_____ в магази́н. (*went*)

5. Ты_____ в Москву́ зимо́й? (*went*)

6. Вче́ра моя́ жена́_____ на по́чту. (*went*)

7. Вче́ра ве́чером мы_____ в рестора́н. (*went*)

B. Say what foreign languages the following people speak because they lived and worked in certain foreign countries. Remember to conjugate the verb говори́ть.

1. Мой друг жил и рабо́тал во Фра́нции. Он хорошо́ _____

    _____.

2. Моя́ жена́ жила́ и рабо́тала в Аргенти́не. Она́ хорошо́ _____

    _____.

3. Джон жил и рабо́тал в Еги́пте. Он хорошо́ _____

    _____.

4. Мы жи́ли и рабо́тали в Ита́лии. Мы немно́го _____

    _____.

5. Мои́ роди́тели жи́ли и рабо́тали в Япо́нии. Они́ непло́хо _____

   _____.

6. Моя́ сестра́ жила́ и рабо́тала в Росси́и. Она́ о́чень хорошо́ _____

   _____.

7. Наш сын жил и рабо́тал в Герма́нии. Он хорошо́ _____

   _____.

C. Now let's practice what you've learned in an audio exercise. Repeat the following
   Russian sentences and then translate them into English.

1. В Росси́и говоря́т по-ру́сски.

   _____

2. Мы е́здили в Росси́ю ле́том.

   _____

3. Моя́ жена́ е́здила в Аме́рику ле́том.

   _____

4. Ле́том мы бы́ли в Аме́рике.

   _____

5. Вы о́чень хорошо́ говори́те по-англи́йски.

   _____

D. Translate the following English sentences into Russian. Say the Russian sentence
   out loud.

1. *Do you (form.) speak English?*

   _____

2. *I went to Moscow in the winter.*

_____

3. *Did they go to St. Petersburg?*

_____

4. *Yesterday, we went to a restaurant.*

_____

5. *In Germany, they speak German.*

_____

ANSWER KEY

A. 1. éздил; 2. éздили; 3. ходи́ли; 4. ходи́ли; 5. éздил; 6. ходи́ла; 7. ходи́ли

B. 1. говори́т по-францу́зски; 2. говори́т по-испа́нски; 3. говори́т по-ара́бски; 4. говори́м по-италья́нски; 5. говоря́т по-япо́нски; 6. говори́т по-ру́сски; 7. говори́т по-неме́цки

C. 1. *They speak Russian in Russia.* 2. *We went to Russia in the summer.* 3. *My wife went to America in the summer.* 4. *In the summer, we were in America.* 5. *You speak English very well.*

D. 1. Вы говори́те по-англи́йски? 2. Я éздил в Москву́ зимо́й. 3. Они́ éздили в Санкт-Петербу́рг? 4. Вчера́ мы ходи́ли в рестора́н. 5. В Герма́нии говоря́т по-неме́цки.

✎ Drive It Home

A. Restate the following sentences, replacing the verb *to be* with the verb *to go* in the past tense. Remember also to change the case from the prepositional case of location to the accusative case of direction as you replace был with ходи́л or éздил.

1. Я был в Москве́.

_____

2. Мы бы́ли в Росси́и.

_____

3. Они́ бы́ли в Аме́рике.

_____

4. Они́ бы́ли в Вашингто́не.

_____

5. Вы бы́ли у́тром в магази́не?

_____

6. Ты был днём на рабо́те?

_____

7. Вы бы́ли ве́чером в кафе́.

_____

8. Где вы бы́ли вчера́?

_____

B. Fill in the blanks using the correct forms of the adjectives in parentheses.

1. Москва́ – _____ и о́чень _____ го́род.

   (old, interesting)

2. Соединённые Шта́ты Аме́рики – _____ страна́. (big)

3. Конне́ктикут – _____ штат. (small)

4. Э́то мой _____ дом. (new)

5. Э́то о́чень _____ кре́сло. (old)

6. Э́то на́ша _____ по́чта. (new)

7. Э́то на́ши _____ ру́сские друзья́. (good)

At a Restaurant

Talking about Past Activities

Talking about Where
You're From

Countries and Languages

Socializing

8. Нью-Йорк – _____ го́род. (*big*)

C. Fill in the blanks using the appropriate languages they speak in the countries below.

1. В Аме́рике говоря́т _____.

2. В Герма́нии говоря́т _____.

3. В Росси́и говоря́т _____.

4. В Ита́лии говоря́т _____.

5. В Аргенти́не говоря́т _____.

6. В Япо́нии говоря́т _____.

7. Во Фра́нции говоря́т _____.

ANSWER KEY
A. 1. Я е́здил в Москву́. 2. Мы е́здили в Росси́ю. 3. Они́ е́здили в Аме́рику. 4. Они́ е́здили в Вашингто́н. 5. Вы ходи́ли у́тром в магази́н? 6. Ты ходи́л днём на рабо́ту? 7. Вы ходи́ли ве́чером в кафе́. 8. Куда́ вы ходи́ли вчера́?
B. 1. ста́рый, интере́сный; 2. больша́я; 3. ма́ленький; 4. но́вый; 5. ста́рое; 6. но́вая; 7. хоро́шие; 8. большо́й
C. 1. по-англи́йски; 2. по-неме́цки; 3. по-ру́сски; 4. по-италья́нски; 5. по-испа́нски; 6. по-япо́нски; 7. по-францу́зски

Parting Words

Congratulations on finishing eight lessons! After this lesson, you should know how to:

☐ Speak about different countries. (Still unsure? Go back to page 141.)

☐ Differentiate between going to a place and being there. (Still unsure? Go back to page 143.)

☐ Use the accusative case of direction. (Still unsure? Go back to page 143.)

☐ Speak about different nationalities and languages. (Still unsure? Go back to page 146.)

☐ Use adjectives in the nominative case. (Still unsure? Go back to page 147.)

Don't forget to practice and reinforce what you've learned by visiting **www.livinglanguage.com/ languagelab** for flashcards, games, and quizzes!

Word Recall

Готóвы? (*Ready?*) Let's review the vocabulary from the eight lessons we've gone through so far. Translate the following sentences using the clues provided to help you with the challenging vocabulary and grammar.

1. *This is an American journalist.* (female) (Remember that American is an adjective.)

   _____

2. *Does this young man speak English?*

   _____

3. *When did you (form.) go to Moscow?*(Remember to use the vehicular motion verb with the accusative case.)

   _____

4. *What did you (inform.) eat and drink for breakfast?* (Remember to use the accusative case.)

   _____

5. *Where do they want (would they like) to have dinner?*

   _____

6. *I'll have soup and salad for lunch.*(Use the verb *to be* in the future tense with the accusative case.)

   _____

7. *This is a very interesting letter.*(Remember that the Russian word for letter is neuter.)

_____

8. *Would you (form.) pass the bread please?*

_____

9. *Where were you [plural] in the summer?*(Remember to use the prepositional case.)

_____

10. *We worked in a firm in New York.*(Remember to use the past tense and the prepositional case.)

_____

ANSWER KEY

1. Это американская журналистка. 2. Этот молодой человек говорит по-английски? 3. Когда вы ездили в Москву? 4. Что ты ел и пил на завтрак? 5. Где они хотят ужинать? 6. Я буду суп и салат на обед. 7. Это очень интересное письмо. 8. Передайте, пожалуйста, хлеб. 9. Где вы были летом? 10. Мы работали на/в фирме в Нью-Йорке.

Essential Russian

Lesson 9: Talking About Past Activities

Девя́тый уро́к: Что вы де́лали?

Как всегда́, мы ра́ды вас ви́деть! *As always, we're glad to see you!* In this lesson, you'll learn how to:

☐ Talk about your activities on different days of the week.

☐ Talk about events in the past tense.

☐ Use adjectives in the prepositional and accusative cases.

☐ Put it all together in a conversation about a regular day at work.

Гото́вы? Тогда́ начнём! *Ready? Then, let's begin!* Let's get started with some new words and phrases.

Vocabulary Builder 1

▶ 9A Vocabulary Builder 1 (CD: 3, Track: 1)

Monday, on Monday	понеде́льник, в понеде́льник
Tuesday, on Tuesday	вто́рник, во вто́рник
Wednesday, on Wednesday	среда́, в сре́ду
Thursday, on Thursday	четве́рг, в четве́рг
Friday, on Friday	пя́тница, в пя́тницу
Saturday, on Saturday	суббо́та, в суббо́ту
Sunday, on Sunday	воскресе́нье, в воскресе́нье
week	неде́ля
What day of the week is today?	Како́й сего́дня день неде́ли?
to do	де́лать
to rest, to vacation	отдыха́ть
to go to the movies	ходи́ть в кино́
weather	пого́да

✎ Vocabulary Practice 1

A. Rearrange the following days of the week from Monday to Sunday. Keep in mind that the Russian week always starts on Monday. Also notice the gender of different days of the week.

четве́рг

пя́тница

воскресе́нье

понеде́льник

вто́рник

среда́

суббо́та

_____

_____

Can you repeat them out loud in order? Try doing so without looking.

B. Fill out the conjugation chart for the following verbs.

1. де́лать (*to do*)

я	
ты	
он, она́	
мы	
вы	
они́	

2. отдыха́ть (*to rest*; *to vacation*)

я	
ты	
он, она́	
мы	
вы	
они́	

ANSWER KEY

A. 1. понеде́льник; 2. вто́рник; 3. среда́; 4. четрве́рг; 5. пя́тница; 6. суббо́та; 7. воскресе́нье

B. 1. де́лаю, де́лаешь, де́лает, де́лаем, де́лаете, де́лают; 2. отдыха́ю, отдыха́ешь, отдыха́ет, отдыха́ем, отдыха́ете, отдыха́ют

Grammar Builder 1

▶ 9B Grammar Builder 1 (CD: 3, Track: 2)

ASKING AND ANSWERING QUESTIONS ABOUT DAYS OF THE WEEK

The question, Какóй сегóдня день недéли? means *What day of the week is today?* Remember that when you ask a question with a question word + noun combination, such as *what day*, you must use the adjectival form of the question word, e.g. какой, какая, какое, or какие. This is different from English, where the question word is the same whether or not it modifies a noun (e.g., *what, what day?*). Notice that the adjectival interrogative agrees with the noun it asks about :

Какóй сегóдня день?
What day is today?

Какáя сегóдня погóда?
What's the weather today?

Какóе сегóдня числó?
What's the date today?, etc.

The answer to such a question can be either a noun:

Какóй сегóдня день?
What day is today?

Сегóдня понедéльник.
Today is Monday.

Or an adjective:

Како́й сего́дня день?
What (kind of) day is today?

Сего́дня хоро́ший день.
Today is a good day.

When you need to say that something happened on a particular day of the week, you need to use the preposition в with the accusative (not prepositional!) case. So you need to say:

В понеде́льник она́ рабо́тала в о́фисе.
On Monday, she worked in the office.

В суббо́ту он отдыха́л до́ма.
On Saturday, he rested/stayed at home.

В воскресе́нье мы ходи́ли в кино́.
On Sunday, we went to the movies.

Remember that all masculine and neuter days of the week stay the same in the accusative case, but feminine ones, such as среда́ and суббо́та have the ending –у: в сре́ду, в суббо́ту.

Vocabulary Builder 2

▶ 9C Vocabulary Builder 2 (CD: 3, Track: 3)

What restaurant did you go to?	В како́й рестора́н вы ходи́ли?
What coffee shop did you go to?	В каку́ю кофе́йню вы ходи́ли?

In what restaurant were you?	В како́м рестора́не вы бы́ли?
In what coffee shop were you?	В како́й кофе́йне вы бы́ли?
What [kind of] cuisine do you like?	Каку́ю ку́хню вы лю́бите?
borshch (Russian beet soup)	борщ
Russian cuisine	ру́сская ку́хня
Italian cuisine	италья́нская ку́хня
French cuisine	францу́зская ку́хня
Japanese cuisine	япо́нская ку́хня
Chinese cuisine	кита́йская ку́хня
Indian cuisine	инди́йская ку́хня
black	чёрный
white	бе́лый
red	кра́сный
green	зелёный

✎ Vocabulary Practice 2

A. Match the following dishes in the left column with the types of cuisine in the right one. These may be new words for you, but you should be able to logically conclude what cuisine the dish belongs to.

1. па́ста   a. францу́зская ку́хня

2. су́ши   b. кита́йская ку́хня

3. борщ   c. инди́йская ку́хня

4. суфле́   d. италья́нская ку́хня

5. ку́рица «Танду́ри»   e. япо́нская ку́хня

6. суп «Ванто́н»   f. ру́сская ку́хня

B. Match the English items in the left column with their Russian equivalents in the right one.

1. *red wine*	a. бе́лое вино́
2. *white bread*	b. чёрный хлеб
3. *green tea*	c. чёрный ко́фе
4. *black bread*	d. бе́лый хлеб
5. *green salad*	e. зелёный чай
6. *white wine*	f. кра́сное вино́
7. *Italian ice cream*	g. ру́сский борщ
8. *Russian borshch*	h. францу́зский десе́рт
9. *French dessert*	i. италья́нское моро́женое
10. *black coffee*	j. зелёный сала́т

ANSWER KEY
A. 1. d; 2. e; 3. f; 4. a; 5. c; 6. b
B. 1. f; 2. d; 3. e; 4. b; 5. j; 6. a; 7. i; 8. g; 9. h; 10. c

Grammar Builder 2
▶ 9D Grammar Builder 2 (CD: 3, Track: 4)

ADJECTIVAL ENDINGS

Notice the difference in the adjectival endings in the questions:

MASCULINE AND NEUTER SINGULAR

В како́м рестора́не вы бы́ли?
In what restaurant were you?

В како́м кафе́ вы бы́ли?
In what café were you?

and

FEMININE SINGULAR

В како́й кофе́йне вы бы́ли?
In what coffee shop were you?

To sum up, the masculine and neuter singular adjectival ending is –ом; the feminine singular adjectival ending is –ой

Мы бы́ли в ру́сском рестора́не.
Мы бы́ли во францу́зском кафе́.
Мы бы́ли в италья́нской кофе́йне.

Now let's learn one more distinction between the prepositional case and the accusative case: masculine singular and neuter singular adjectives (modifying inanimate nouns) stay the same in the accusative case as in the nominative; the feminine singular adjectives (modifying animate or inanimate nouns) have the ending –ую (the feminine nouns they modify have the ending –у). For example, you should say:

Мы ходи́ли в ру́сский рестора́н.
We went to a Russian restaurant.

Мы ходи́ли во францу́зское кафе́.
We went to a French café.

Мы ходи́ли в италья́нскую кофе́йню.
We went to an Italian coffee shop.

Я люблю́ кита́йскую ку́хню.
I like Chinese cuisine.

✎ Work Out 1

▶ 9F Work Out 1 (CD: X, Track Y)

Now let's review some of the new grammar and vocabulary. As usual you'll hear the English first, then fill in the missing Russian words, and finally, repeat the correct answers in the pauses provided.

Example: *What did you do this week?*
Что вы де́лали на э́той неде́ле?

1. *On Monday, we went to the movies.*

   В понеде́льник мы _____.

2. *On Tuesday, she went to a Russian restaurant.*

   Во вто́рник она́ ходи́ла _____.

3. *On Saturday, they were in a Japanese restaurant.*

   В суббо́ту они́ бы́ли _____.

4. *My children like Chinese cuisine.*

   Мои́ де́ти лю́бят _____.

5. *This is a good Italian restaurant.*

   Э́то хоро́ший _____ рестора́н.

6. *He was in a new café on Wednesday.*

   Он был в _____ кафе́.

7. *I like red wine.*

   Я люблю́ _____ вино́.

8. *They like Russian cuisine.*

Они́ лю́бят _____.

9. *What (kind of) cuisine do you like?*

_____ ку́хню вы лю́бите?

10. *They had breakfast in a French coffee shop.*

Они́ за́втракали во _____.

ANSWER KEY
1. ходи́ли в кино́; 2. в ру́сский рестора́н; 3. в япо́нском рестора́не; 4. кита́йскую ку́хню;
5. италья́нский; 6. сре́ду в но́вом; 7. кра́сное; 8. ру́сскую ку́хню; 9. Каку́ю; 10. францу́зской
кофе́йне

⊕ Bring It All Together

▶ 9F Bring It All Together (CD: 3, Track: 6)

Now let's listen to a dialogue that highlights the structures and phrases from this
lesson. Listen to Irina asking Eric about his week.

Irina:	*Eric, what did you do on Saturday? Did you work?*
Ири́на:	Э́рик, что ты де́лал в суббо́ту? Ты рабо́тал?
Eric:	*No, on Saturday, my friends and I (lit., we with friends) went to a Russian restaurant.*
Э́рик:	Нет, в суббо́ту мы с друзья́ми ходи́ли в ру́сский рестора́н.
Irina:	*Do you like Russian cuisine?*
Ири́на:	Ты лю́бишь ру́сскую ку́хню?
Eric:	*Not really, but I like borshch and black bread. And what did you do on Saturday and Sunday, Irina?*
Эри́к:	Не о́чень, но я люблю́ борщ и чёрный хлеб. А что ты де́лала в суббо́ту и в воскресе́нье, Ири́на?
Irina:	*I was at home, I also rested. Then, I went to the movies and walked a lot on Sunday.*

Ири́на:	Я была́ до́ма, я то́же отдыха́ла. Пото́м я ходи́ла в кино́ и мно́го гуля́ла в воскресе́нье.
Eric:	*Yes, the weather on Sunday was very good. Did you have lunch in the city?*
Э́рик:	Да, в воскре́сенье была́ о́чень хоро́шая пого́да. Ты обе́дала в го́роде?
Irina:	*No, I didn't go to a restaurant but I went to a new Italian coffee shop.*
Ири́на:	Нет, я не ходи́ла в рестора́н, но я ходи́ла в но́вую италья́нскую кофе́йню.
Eric:	*(That's) good for you, but I worked in the office on Sunday.*
Э́рик:	Молоде́ц, а я рабо́тал в о́фисе в воскресе́нье.

Take It Further 1

You're learning more and more vocabulary with each lesson. Let's sum up the new words used in the conversation above.

Мы с друзья́ми (*my friends and I*) is an idiomatic phrase that literally translates as *we with friends*. It employs a plural pronoun and a noun, друзья́ми, in the instrumental plural case, which you'll learn later. For now, just remember it as it is.

Пото́м (*then*) is an adverb. It's used much like its English equivalent except that it doesn't require a comma.

Молоде́ц (*good job, good for you, lucky you*, etc.) is a word of admiration or praise equally applied to women and men. Its plural form is молодцы́.

Не о́чень (*not really, not that much*) is a common colloquial phrase.

✎ Work Out 2

▶ 9G Work Out 2 (CD: 3, Track 7)

A. Answer the following questions using the adjectives in parentheses. Notice that the adjectives are given in the "dictionary form," i.e., in the nominative masculine singular, but remember to make them agree in case, gender, and number with the nouns they modify.

1. Кака́я сего́дня пого́да? (хоро́ший)

2. Каку́ю ку́хню вы лю́бите? (италья́нский)

3. В како́м рестора́не мы бы́ли в пя́тницу? (кита́йский)

4. В каку́ю кофе́йню они́ ходи́ли в четве́рг? (францу́зский)

5. В како́е кафе́ вы (pl.) всегда́ хо́дите? (но́вый)

6. В како́м кафе́ вы (pl.) обы́чно обе́даете? (но́вый)

7. Како́й чай вы (fml.) лю́бите? (чёрный)

8. Како́е вино́ мы бу́дем пить на у́жин? (бе́лый)

9. Кака́я вчера́ была́ пого́да? (плохо́й)

   _____

10. В како́м го́роде ты живёшь? (ма́ленький)

   _____

B. And now listen to your audio for some more practice. Repeat the following Russian sentences and then translate them into English.

1. Како́й сего́дня день неде́ли?

   _____

2. Сего́дня пя́тница.

   _____

3. В суббо́ту мы ходи́ли в ру́сский рестора́н.

   _____

4. Я люблю́ ру́сскую ку́хню.

   _____

5. Мы ча́сто обе́даем в кита́йском рестора́не.

   _____

C. Translate the following English sentences you'll hear into Russian. Say the Russian sentence out loud.

1. *What did you (inform.) do on Sunday?*

   _____

2. *On Sunday, we went to the movies.*

   _____

3. *On Wednesday, the weather was good.*

   _____

4. *She had lunch in an Italian restaurant.*

   _____

5. *Do they like Russian cuisine?*

   _____

ANSWER KEY

A. 1. Сего́дня хоро́шая пого́да. 2. Я люблю́ италья́нскую ку́хню. 3. В пя́тницу мы бы́ли в кита́йском рестора́не. 4. В четве́рг они́ ходи́ли во францу́зскую кофе́йню. 5. Мы всегда́ хо́дим в но́вое кафе́. 6. Мы обы́чно обе́даем в но́вом кафе́. 7. Я люблю́ чёрный чай. 8. Мы бу́дем пить бе́лое вино́ на у́жин. 9. Вчера́ была́ плоха́я пого́да. 10. Я живу́ в ма́леньком го́роде.

B. 1. *What day of the week is today?* 2. *Today is Friday.* 3. *On Saturday, we went to a Russian restaurant.* 4. *I like Russian cuisine.* 5. *We often have lunch at a Chinese restaurant.*

C. 1. Что ты де́лал в воскресе́нье? 2. В воскресе́нье мы ходи́ли в кино́. 3. В сре́ду пого́да была́ хоро́шая. 4. Она́ обе́дала в италья́нском рестора́не. 5. Они́ лю́бят ру́сскую ку́хню.

✎ Drive It Home

A. Say what you do on the following days of the week. Remember to put the days of the week into the accusative case.

1. Сего́дня вто́рник. _____ я рабо́таю в о́фисе.

2. Сего́дня среда́. _____ я обе́даю в кита́йском рестора́не.

3. Сего́дня пя́тница. _____ я обы́чно ве́чером хожу́ в кафе́.

4. Сего́дня суббо́та. _____ я ча́сто хожу́ в кино́.

5. Сего́дня воскресе́нье. _____ я всегда́ отдыха́ю до́ма.

B. Finish the second sentence with the cuisine of the restaurant mentioned in the first sentence. Be sure to say the sentences out loud.

1. Мы бы́ли в инди́йском рестора́не. Мы лю́бим _____

    _____.

2. Мы бы́ли в ру́сском рестора́не. Мы лю́бим _____.

3. Мы бы́ли во францу́зском рестора́не. Мы лю́бим _____

    _____.

4. Мы бы́ли в япо́нском рестора́не. Мы лю́бим _____.

5. Мы бы́ли в италья́нском рестора́не. Мы лю́бим _____

    _____.

C. Replace the verb *to be* (был/была́/бы́ли) with the verb *to go* (ходи́л/ходила/ ходи́ли) in the past tense. Remember to change the case of the nouns and adjectives as you change location to direction.

1. В сре́ду мы бы́ли в италья́нском кафе́.

    _____

2. Во вто́рник они́ бы́ли во францу́зской кофе́йне.

    _____

3. В понеде́льник я была́ в кита́йском рестора́не.

    _____

4. В воскресе́нье он был в инди́йском рестора́не.

    _____

5. В суббо́ту ты был в но́вом кафе́.

ANSWER KEY

A. 1. Во вто́рник; **2.** В сре́ду; **3.** В пя́тницу; **4.** В суббо́ту; **5.** В воскресе́нье
B. 1. инди́йскую ку́хню; **2.** ру́сскую ку́хню; **3.** францу́зскую ку́хню; **4.** япо́нскую ку́хню;
5. италья́нскую ку́хню
C. 1. В сре́ду мы ходи́ли в италья́нское кафе́. **2.** Во вто́рник они́ ходи́ли во францу́зскую
кофе́йню. **3.** В понеде́льник я ходи́ла в кита́йский рестора́н. **4.** В воскресе́нье он ходи́л в
инди́йский рестора́н. **5.** В суббо́ту ты ходи́л в но́вое кафе́.

Take It Further 2

Negation in Russian is very simple. As you've seen in the dialogue, the word for *no* is нет. Не is a negative particle that negates any word it immediately precedes:

Я не люблю́ ру́сскую ку́хню.
I don't like Russian cuisine.

This is the most common position of this negative particle—before the verb. However, it can be put anywhere in the sentence with the following changes of meaning:

Я люблю́ не ру́сскую ку́хню, а япо́нскую.
It's not Russian cuisine that I like, but Japanese.

or

Не я люблю́ ру́сскую ку́хню, а моя́ сестра́.
I'm not the one who likes Russian cuisine, but rather my sister is.

As you can see, changing the position of the negative particle changes what is negated (e.g. who does the liking or what is liked).

Parting Words

Well done! Now, you should know how to:

☐ Talk about your activities on different days of the week. (Still unsure? Go back to page 160.)

☐ Use adjectives in the prepositional and accusative cases. (Still unsure? Go back to page 166.)

☐ Talk about events in the past tense. (Still unsure? Go back to page 168.)

☐ Put it all together in a conversation about a regular day at work. (Still unsure? Go back to page 168.)

Don't forget to practice and reinforce what you've learned by visiting **www.livinglanguage.com/languagelab** for flashcards, games, and quizzes!

Word Recall

Гото́вы? (*Ready?*) Let's review some of the vocabulary from the nine lessons we've gone through so far. Match the English phrases in the right column with their equivalents on the left.

1. два су́па	a. *we lived/stayed at a hotel*
2. на десе́рт	b. *good-bye*
3. на у́жин	c. *as an appetizer*
4. в торго́вом це́нтре	d. *where are you from*
5. э́то мои́ де́ти	e. *in the mall*
6. на заку́ску	f. *for dessert*
7. три ко́мнаты	g. *where do you live*
8. отку́да вы	h. *two soups*
9. я из Аме́рики	i. *these are my children*
10. где вы живёте	j. *three rooms*
11. мы жи́ли в гости́нице	k. *for dinner*
12. до свида́ния	l. *I'm from America*

ANSWER KEY
1. h; 2. f; 3. k; 4. e; 5. i; 6. c; 7. j; 8. d; 9. l; 10. g; 11. a; 12. b

Lesson 10: Socializing

Деся́тый уро́к: Что у вас есть?

Поздравля́ем с нача́лом после́днего уро́ка ку́рса *Essential Russian*!
Congratulations on beginning the final lesson of Essential Russian! In this lesson,
you'll learn how to:

☐ Talk about possessions.

☐ Ask how a person is doing.

☐ Say that you have a lot or a little of something.

☐ Say that your are busy.

☐ Talk about what floor one lives on.

☐ Use cardinal and ordinal numbers from 1 to 10.

☐ Put it all together in a conversation.

Гото́вы? Тогда́ начнём! *Ready? Then, let's begin!* Let's get started with some
new words and phrases.

Vocabulary Builder 1

⏵ 10A Vocabulary Builder 1 (CD: 3, Track: 8)

I have a dog	у меня́ есть соба́ка
you (inform.) have a dog	у тебя́ есть соба́ка
he has a dog	у него́ есть соба́ка
she has a dog	у неё есть соба́ка
we have a dog	у нас есть соба́ка
you have a dog	у вас есть соба́ка
they have a dog	у них есть соба́ка
gym (sports hall)	спорти́вный зал
swimming pool	бассе́йн
metro, subway	метро́
car	маши́на
floor, story	эта́ж
garden	сад
vegetable garden	огоро́д
flowers	цветы́
cat	ко́шка

✎ Vocabulary Practice 1

A. Let's practice the new vocabulary. Match the personal pronouns on the left with the corresponding expressions of possession on the right.

1. я	a. У нас есть соба́ка.
2. мы	b. У неё есть соба́ка.
3. вы	c. У тебя́ есть соба́ка.
4. они́	d. У меня́ есть соба́ка.
5. он	e. У вас есть соба́ка.
6. ты	f. У них есть соба́ка.
7. она́	g. У него́ есть соба́ка.

B. Match the English words and expressions on the left with the Russian words and expressions on the right.

1. *gym*	a. соба́ка
2. *cat*	b. метро́
3. *dog*	c. огоро́д
4. *floor*	d. маши́на
5. *swimming pool*	e. ко́шка
6. *flowers*	f. спорти́вный зал
7. *garden*	g. эта́ж
8. *car*	h. цветы́
9. *vegetable garden*	i. сад
10. *metro*	j. бассе́йн

ANSWER KEY
A. 1. d; 2. a; 3. e; 4. f; 5. g; 6. c; 7. b
B. 1. f; 2. e; 3. a; 4. g; 5. j; 6. h; 7. i; 8. d; 9. c; 10. b

Grammar Builder 1

▶ 10C Grammar Builder 1 (CD: 3, Track: 9)

EXPRESSING POSSESSION IN RUSSIAN

У меня́ есть соба́ка means *I have a dog*. This construction is a standard way of expressing possession in Russian. This is how it works. First, you should use the preposition у with the personal pronoun or noun referring to the possessor in the genitive case, which literally translates as "by x." Then, you have the verb *to be*—есть—the one we normally omit in the present tense. This verb stays the same in the present tense for all persons and numbers. And finally you have the object of possession, which doesn't change: it always remains in the nominative case. So, rather than saying that *I have a dog*, in Russian we say, "*By me is a dog.*"

У + GENITIVE	THE VERB *TO BE*	NOMINATIVE (SG. OR PLURAL)
у меня́	есть	соба́ка, ко́шка, муж, жена́, дом, кварти́ра, де́ти, друзья́, *etc.*
у тебя́		
у него́		
у неё		
у нас		
у них		

Take It Further 1

The verb *to be*—есть—can and should be omitted from the above construction when the emphasis is not on the fact of possession but on a particular quality of the possessed object or when you locate the object with a particular possessor. For example: У нас хоро́шие де́ти means that *We have good kids* (the emphasis is not on the fact that we have children but that our children are good). У нас твоя́ соба́ка means that *We have your dog* (you've been looking for your dog, but don't worry we have it).

Vocabulary Builder 2

▶ 10C Vocabulary Builder 2 (CD: 3, Track: 10)

How are you doing? (inform./form.)	Как у тебя́/у вас дела́?
What do you have? (inform./form.)	Что у тебя́/у вас есть?
What is today's date?	Како́е сего́дня число́?
first	пе́рвый
second	второ́й
third	тре́тий
fourth	четвёртый
So long! Take care! (inform.)	Пока́!
a lot of things (to do)	мно́го дел
little time	ма́ло вре́мени
he is busy, she is busy, they are busy	он за́нят, она́ занята́, они́ за́няты
great, excellent	отли́чно

✎ Vocabulary Practice 2

A. Rearrange the following ordinal numerals in ascending order.
   второ́й, четвёртый, пе́рвый, тре́тий

_____

_____

B. Match the English expressions on the left with the corresponding Russian equivalents on the right.

1. *lots of things to do*   a. отли́чно

2. *little time*   b. э́тот дом

3. *How are you doing?*   c. Како́е сего́дня число́?

4. *So long!*   d. мно́го дел

5. *he is busy*   e. Как у вас дела́?

6. *What date is today?*   f. ма́ло вре́мени

7. *excellent, great*   g. Пока́!

8. *this house*   h. он за́нят

ANSWER KEY
A. пе́рвый, второ́й, тре́тий, четвёртый
B. 1. d; 2. f; 3. e; 4. g; 5. h; 6. c; 7. a; 8. b

Grammar Builder 2
(▶) 10D Grammar Builder 2 (CD: 3, Track: 11)

TALKING ABOUT ONE'S STATE OF BEING AND THE DATE

Как у вас дела́?—literally translates as *How are things by you?* The noun дела́ (*things*) is the plural form of the neuter noun де́ло (*thing, business, affair, case*). The verb is omitted in this construction because the emphasis is not on possession but rather on its quality—*how*. The standard answers to this question vary. The following table gives you some possible answers from excellent to bad. Notice that while in English you might use an adjective in these responses, the Russian equivalents are adverbs:

great, excellent	отли́чно
very well	о́чень хорошо́
not bad at all	неплохо́
not so well	не о́чень

so-so	та́к себе
bad(ly)	пло́хо
very bad(ly)	о́чень пло́хо
terribl(y)	ужа́сно

When it's your turn to ask how someone is doing in response to his or her question, you need to replicate the same structure that was in the original question. You should say: А у вас? (*And you? [form.]*) or А у тебя? (*And you? [inform.]*) but not "А вы?" As an example, read and memorize the following exchange:

Как у вас дела́?
How are you doing?

Хорошо́. А у вас?
(I'm) Well. And you?

Спаси́бо, у меня́ то́же хорошо́.
Thank you, I'm well too.

Како́е сего́дня число́? means *What is today's date?* The noun число́ is neuter singular, therefore the adjectival question word како́е (*what, which*) is also neuter and singular and so are the actual dates in the possible answers. So you should say:

Сего́дня пе́рвое.
Today is the first.

Сего́дня второ́е.
Today is the second.

Сего́дня тре́тье.
Today is the third.

Сего́дня четве́ртое.
Today is the fourth.

The noun число́ (*date*) must be omitted in the answer. Below is the chart with cardinal numerals from 1 to 10 (you already know the first four) and their corresponding ordinals from 1 to 10 in the nominative masculine singular form (the dictionary form). Be aware that the actual endings of Russian ordinals are standard adjectival endings; as such, they agree in number, gender, and case with the nouns they modify as all other adjectives do. Only the ordinal тре́тий, тре́тье, тре́тья, тре́тьи (*third*) is irregular and needs to be memorized.

оди́н	пе́рвый	*first*
два	второ́й	*second*
три	тре́тий	*third*
четы́ре	четвёртый	*fourth*
пять	пя́тый	*fifth*
ше́сть	шесто́й	*sixth*
семь	седьмо́й	*seventh*
во́семь	восьмо́й	*eighth*
де́вять	девя́тый	*ninth*
де́сять	деся́тый	*tenth*

✎ Work Out 1
▶ 10E Work Out 1 (CD: 3, Track: 12)

Now let's practice! You'll hear the English first, and then the Russian, which you should repeat for practice.

1. *How are you (form.) doing?*

   Как_____ дела́?

2. *I'm doing great! And you (form.)?*

   У меня́_____! _____? *Do they have a car?*

   _____маши́на? *I want (I'd like) a new car.*

   Я хочу́_____.

3. *We have a house and a garden.*

   _____есть дом и _____.

4. *What is today's date?*

   Како́е сего́дня_____?

5. *Today is the fourth.*

   Сего́дня _____.

6. *He is very busy today. He has little time.*

   Он о́чень _____ сего́дня. _____ ма́ло вре́мени.

7. *What floor does she live on?*

   _____этаже́ она́ живёт?

8. *She lives on the seventh floor.*

   Она́ живёт _____ этаже́.

ANSWER KEY

1. у вас; 2. отли́чно, А у вас; 3. У них есть; 4. но́вую маши́ну; 5. У нас, сад; 6. число́; 7. четвёртое; 8. за́нят, У него́; 9. На како́м; 10. на седьмо́м

🎧 Bring It All Together

▶ 10F Bring It All Together (CD: 3, Track: 13)

Now let's bring it all together and listen to a dialogue that highlights the structures and phrases from this lesson. Tanya and Bill, who live in the same apartment building, run into each other in the elevator.

Tanya:	*Hey, Bill, how are you doing?*
Та́ня:	Приве́т, Билл! Как у тебя́ дела́?
Bill:	*(I'm) fine, Tanya, but I'm so busy! I have a lot of things (to do).*
Билл:	Хорошо́, Та́ня, но я так за́нят! У меня́ мно́го дел.
Tanya:	*What are you doing? (What do you need to do?)*
Та́ня:	Что ты де́лаешь?
Bill:	*I have a lot to do at work, but don't have much time (lit., have little time). And how are you doing, Tanya?*
Билл:	У меня́ мно́го дел на рабо́те, а вре́мени ма́ло. А как у тебя́ дела́, Та́ня?
Tanya:	*I'm doing great (lit., everything is great by me), but I'm very busy too.*
Та́ня:	У меня́ всё отли́чно, но я то́же о́чень занята́.
Bill:	*And what do you have?*
Билл:	А что у тебя́?
Tanya:	*You know, we have a new dog.*
Та́ня:	Зна́ешь, у нас но́вая соба́ка.
Bill:	*Congratulations!*
Билл:	Поздравля́ю!
Tanya:	*Thanks.*
Та́ня:	Спаси́бо!
Bill:	*You're on the fourth floor, right?*

Билл:	Ты на четвёртом этаже́, да?
Tanya:	*Yes. And you're on the eighth?*
Та́ня:	Да. А ты на восьмо́м?
Bill:	*Yes, on the eighth. Well, here's your floor.*
Билл:	Да, на восьмом. Ну, вот и твой эта́ж.
Tanya:	*See you soon, Bill!*
Та́ня:	До ско́рого, Билл!
Bill:	*So long, Tanya!*
Билл:	Пока́, Та́ня!

Take It Further 2

The expression, *I am busy* (я за́нят/занята́), agrees in gender and number with the gender and number of the subject. This is how it works:

Он за́нят.
He is busy.

Она́ занята́.
She is busy.

Они́ за́няты.
They are busy.

The adverbs мно́го (*a lot*) and ма́ло (*little, few*) take a noun in the genitive case—the genitive singular if the following noun doesn't have the plural form, e.g. ма́ло вре́мени (*little time*) or the genitive plural if the following noun has the plural form, e.g., мно́го дел (*a lot of things*). We'll cover the genitive plural and the declension (inflection) of the irregular noun вре́мя (*time*) in Intermediate Russian; for now, just remember these expressions as they are.

Work Out 2

▶ 10G Work Out 2 (CD: 3, Track: 14)

A. Now it's time for some written practice. Answer the following questions using the prompts in parentheses. Remember to put the noun in the prepositional case.
   Example: На како́м этаже́ вы живёте?
   What floor do you live on? (form.)

1. Я живу́_____ этаже́. (второ́й)

2. Я живу́_____ этаже́. (пе́рвый)

3. Я живу́_____ этаже́. (тре́тий)

4. Я живу́_____ этаже́. (четвёртый)

5. Я живу́_____ этаже́. (восьмо́й)

6. Я живу́_____ этаже́. (деся́тый)

B. Read the English sentence first, then fill in the blank, and repeat the Russian sentence out loud.

1. *We have a new gym.*

   У насно́вый _____.

2. *She has a nice garden.*

   _____хоро́ший сад.

3. *Do you (form.) have a dog or cat?*

   _____ соба́ка или ко́шка?

4. *They are very busy.*

   Они́ о́чень _____.

5. *What is today's date?*

   _____ сего́дня число́?

6. *Today is the fourth.*

   Сего́дня _____.

7. *How is she doing?*

   Как у неё _____?

8. *She has a lot of things (to do).*

   У неё _____.

C. Now listen to your audio for additional practice. Repeat the following Russian sentences and then translate them into English.

1. У тебя́ есть маши́на?

   _____

2. Да, у меня́ но́вая америка́нская маши́на.

   _____

3. На како́м этаже́ вы живёте?

   _____

4. Мы живём на пя́том этаже́.

   _____

5. Извини́те, я сего́дня о́чень занята́.

   _____

Lesson 10: Socializing   189

D. Listen to the following English sentences and translate them into Russian. Say the Russian sentences out loud.

1. *What is today's date?*

   _____

2. *Today is the third.*

   _____

3. *Excuse me, I have a lot of things (to do).*

   _____

4. *We have little time.*

   _____

5. *They have a good gym.*

   _____

ANSWER KEY

A. 1. на второ́м; 2. на пе́рвом; 3. на тре́тьем; 4. на четвёртом; 5. на восьмо́м; 6. на деся́том

B. 1. спорти́вный зал; 2. У неё; 3. У вас есть; 4. за́няты; 5. Како́е; 6. четвёртое; 7. дела́; 8. мно́го дел

C. 1. *Do you (inform.) have a car?* 2. *Yes, I have a new American car.* 3. *What floor do you live on?* 4. *We live on the fifth floor.* 5. *Excuse me, I'm very busy today.*

D. 1. Како́е сего́дня число́? 2. Сего́дня тре́тье. 3. Извини́те, у меня́ мно́го дел. 4. У нас ма́ло вре́мени. 5. У них хоро́ший спорти́вный зал.

✎ Drive It Home

A. Let's review some more of the grammar points we've covered in this lesson. Remember to write and read your responses. Fill in the blanks with appropriate possessive pronouns in the genitive case.

1. У _____ есть ко́шка. (я)

2. У _____ есть сад. (мы)

3. У _____ есть спорти́вный зал. (они́)

4. У _____ есть соба́ка. (он)

5. У _____ есть де́ти. (она́)

6. У _____ есть бассе́йн. (вы)

7. У _____ есть маши́на. (ты)

B. Answer the following question using the ordinal numerals in the parentheses. Remember to make them agree with the implied noun число́ (*date*).

Како́е сего́дня число́?

What is today's date?

1. Сего́дня _____.(пе́рвый)

2. Сего́дня _____.(шесто́й)

3. Сего́дня _____.(тре́тий)

4. Сего́дня _____. (четвёртый)

5. Сего́дня _____.(седьмо́й)

6. Сего́дня _____.(девя́тый)

7. Сего́дня _____.(второ́й)

ANSWER KEY

A. 1. меня́; 2. нас; 3. них; 4. него́; 5. неё; 6. вас; 7. тебя́

B. 1. пе́рвое; 2. шесто́е; 3. тре́тье; 4. четвёртое; 5. седьмо́е; 6. девя́тое; 7. второ́е

Parting Words

Congratulations! You've completed the final lesson of *Essential Russian*. Now, you know how to:

☐ Talk about possessions. (Still unsure? Go back to pages 178 and 179.)

☐ Ask how a person is doing. (Still unsure? Go back to page 181.)

☐ Say that your are busy. (Still unsure? Go back to page 181.)

☐ Use cardinal and ordinal numbers from 1 to 10. (Still unsure? Go back to page 184.)

☐ Talk about what floor one lives on. (Still unsure? Go back to page 186.)

☐ Say that you have a lot or a little of something. (Still unsure? Go back to page 187.)

Don't forget to practice and reinforce what you've learned by visiting **www.livinglanguage.com/languagelab** for flashcards, games, and quizzes!

Word Recall

Let's go back and look at the vocabulary you've learned in this program. First, translate the following English expressions into Russian and then repeat them out loud.

1. *What day of the week is today?*

    _____

2. *Today is Friday.*

    _____

3. *On Wednesday, she went to the movies.*

    _____

4. *We had lunch at an Italian restaurant.*

    _____

5. *I like green tea.*

    _____

6. *He vacationed in Russia in the summer.*

    _____

7. *Do you (form.) speak Russian?*

    _____

8. *We'll have orange juice for breakfast.*

    _____

9. *What would you (form.) like for dinner?*

_____

10. **They are from Russia, from St. Petersburg.**

_____

Quiz 2

Контро́льная рабо́та №2

Now let's review. In this section you'll find the second quiz, testing you on what you've learned in Lessons 6–10. Once you've completed it, score yourself to see how well you've done. If you find that you need to go back and review, please do so before continuing on to the final section with review dialogues and comprehension questions.

Let's get started!

A. Answer the question below with a complete sentence, using the season given.

Когда́ вы бы́ли в Росси́и?
When were you in Russia?

1. Я был в Росси́и_____. *(in the summer)*

2. Мы бы́ли в Москве́_____. *(in the fall)*

3. Я была́ в Петербу́рге_____. *(in the spring)*

4. Вы бы́ли в Росси́и_____. *(in the winter)*

B. Say where these people are from.

Отку́да вы? Отку́да они́?

1. *I am from America.*

2. *We are from New York.*

_____

3. *They are from Petersburg.*

_____

4. *He is from Moscow.*

_____

5. *She is from Russia.*

_____

C. Say where these people were.

1. Мы бы́ли вчера́_____. *(a new restaurant)*

2. Она́ была́_____. *(a new post office)*

3. Я был вчера́_____. *(a gym)*

4. Вы бы́ли_____. *(an old town)*

5. Он был_____. *(an Italian coffee shop)*

D. Write what languages are spoken in the following countries.

1. В Росси́и говоря́т _____.

2. В Аме́рике говоря́т _____.

3. Во Фра́нции говоря́т _____.

4. В Япо́нии говоря́т _____.

5. В Еги́пте говоря́т _____.

E. Say where these people went.

1. Билл ходи́л _____ . (the mall)

2. Мы е́здили _____ . (Russia)

3. Утром она́ ходи́ла _____ . (work)

4. Ве́чером он ходи́л _____ . (a French café)

5. Они́ е́здили _____ . (America)

F. Fill in the blanks with the appropriate Russian expression.

1. *I like Japanese cuisine.*

   Я_____ япо́нскую ку́хню.

2. *They like going to the movies.*

   Они́_____ ходи́ть в кино́.

3. *I want to live in a big city.*

   Я _____ жи́ть в большо́м го́роде.

4. *I have Russian friends.*

   _____ ру́сские друзья́.

5. *I often vacation at the Black Sea.*

   Я ча́сто _____ на Чёрном мо́ре.

6. *We will work at home on Saturday.*

   Мы бу́дем рабо́тать до́ма_____ .

7. *How are you doing?* (fml.)

   Как _____ дела́?

ANSWER KEY
A. 1. ле́том; 2. о́сенью; 3. весно́й; 4. зимо́й
B. 1. Я из Аме́рики. 2. Мы из Нью-Йо́рка. 3. Они́ из Петербу́рга. 4. Он из Москвы́.
5. Она́ из Росси́и.

C. 1. в но́вом рестора́не; 2. на но́вой по́чте; 3. в спорти́вном за́ле; 4. в ста́ром го́роде; 5. в италья́нской кофе́йне
D. 1. по-ру́сски; 2. по-англи́йски; 3. по-францу́зски; 4. по-япо́нски; 5. по-ара́бски
E. 1. в торго́вый центр; 2. в Росси́ю; 3. на рабо́ту; 4. во францу́зское кафе́; 5. в Аме́рику
F. 1. люблю́; 2. лю́бят; 3. хочу́; 4. У меня́ есть; 5. отдыха́ю; 6. в суббо́ту; 7. у вас

How Did You Do?

Give yourself a point for every correct answer, then use the following key to determine whether or not you're ready to move on:

0–10 points: It's probably best to go back and study the lessons again to make sure you understood everything completely. Take your time; it's not a race! Make sure you spend time reviewing the vocabulary and reading through each Grammar Builder section carefully.

11–18 points: If the questions you missed were in sections A, D, or E, you may want to review the appropriate vocabulary and conjugations from previous lessons again; if you missed answers mostly in sections B, C, or F, check the Grammar Builder sections to make sure you have your grammar basics down.

19–25 points: Now you're ready to move on to Intermediate Russian. You're doing a great job!

points

Review Dialogues
Welcome!

Добро́ пожа́ловать! *Welcome*!

Here's your chance to practice all the vocabulary and grammar you've mastered in ten lessons of *Living Language Essential Russian* with these five everyday dialogues. Each dialogue is followed by comprehension questions. To practice your pronunciation, don't forget to listen to the audio. You'll hear the dialogue in Russian only, first. Then you'll hear it in Russian and English. Next, for practice, you'll do some role play by taking part in the conversation yourself!

First, try to read the whole dialogue in Russian. Then read and listen to the Russian and English together. How much did you understand? Next, take part in the role play exercise in the audio and answer the comprehension questions here in the book.

Note that there will be words and phrases in these dialogues that you haven't seen yet. This is because we want to give you the feel of a real Russian conversation. As a result, feel free to use your dictionary or the glossary if you're unclear about anything you see. And of course, you'll see the English translations for each line as well.

ⓒ Dialogue 1
МОЯ СЕМЬЯ
MY FAMILY

▶ 11A Dialogue 1 Russian Only (CD: 3, Track 15), 11B Dialogue 1 Russian and English (CD: 3, Track 16), 11C Dialogue 1 Role Play exercise (CD: 3, Track 17)

Emily shows her family photograph to her Russian colleague, Oleg, and tells him about her family.

Э́мили:	Вот, посмотри́те, Оле́г, на э́той фотогра́фии моя́ семья́.
Emily:	*Look, Oleg, here's my family in this photograph.*
Оле́г:	Э́то ва́ши де́ти? А как их зову́т?
Oleg:	*Are these your children? What are their names?*
Э́мили:	Ма́льчика зову́т Зак, а де́вочку зову́т Ре́йчел.
Emily:	*The boy's name is Zack and the girl's name is Rachel.*
Оле́г:	Они́ шко́льники?
Oleg:	*Are they schoolchildren?*
Э́мили:	Да, Зак во второ́м кла́ссе, а Ре́йчел в четвёртом.
Emily:	*Yes, Zack is in second grade and Rachel is in fourth.*
Оле́г:	А э́то в кре́сле ваш муж?
Oleg:	*And is that your husband in the armchair?*
Э́мили:	Да, э́то Крис, мой муж. Он экономи́ст.
Emily:	*Yes, that's Chris, my husband. He's an economist.*
Оле́г:	А где он рабо́тает?
Oleg:	*And where does he work?*
Э́мили:	Он рабо́тает в большо́й фи́рме в Нью-Йо́рке. Он то́же говори́т по-ру́сски.
Emily:	*He works in a big company in New York. He also speaks Russian.*
Оле́г:	Он когда́-нибудь был в Росси́и?
Oleg:	*Has he ever been to Russia?*
Э́мили:	Нет, не был, но, мо́жет быть, он бу́дет в Москве́ весно́й!

Emily:	*No, he hasn't, but maybe he'll be in Moscow in the spring!*
Олег:	Отли́чно! Я бу́ду о́чень рад познако́миться. А э́то ва́ши роди́тели?
Oleg:	*Great! I'll be very glad to meet (him). And are these your parents?*
Э́мили:	Нет, мои́ роди́тели живу́т в Калифо́рнии. А э́то роди́тели моего́ му́жа. Они́ живу́т недалеко́, в шта́те Конне́ктикут.
Emily:	*No, my parents live in California. But these are my husband's parents. They live nearby in the state of Connecticut.*
Олег:	У вас прекра́сная семья́, Э́мили!
Oleg:	*You have a wonderful family, Emily!*
Э́мили:	Большо́е спаси́бо, Оле́г! Я о́чень скуча́ю по ним!
Emily:	*Thank you very much, Oleg! I miss them a lot!*

✏ Dialogue 1 Practice

Now let's check your comprehension of the dialogue and review what you learned in Lessons 1–10. Гото́вы? (Ready?)

1. Кто на фотогра́фии Э́мили?

   _____

2. Как зову́т ма́льчика?

   _____

3. Как зову́т де́вочку?

   _____

4. В како́м кла́ссе её сын?

   _____

5. В како́м кла́ссе её дочь?

   _____

6. Кто муж Э́мили?

_____

7. Где он рабо́тает?

_____

8. Он говори́т по-ру́сски?

_____

9. Он был когда́-нибудь в Росси́и?

_____

10. Когда́, мо́жет быть, он бу́дет в Росси́и?

_____

11. Где живу́т роди́тели Э́мили?

_____

12. Чьи роди́тели на фотогра́фии?

_____

13. Где они́ живу́т?

_____

ANSWER KEY

1. На фотогра́фии де́ти и муж Э́мили и роди́тели её му́жа. 2. Ма́льчика зову́т Зак.
3. Де́вочку зову́т Ре́йчел. 4. Её сын во второ́м кла́ссе. 5. Её дочь в четвёртом кла́ссе.
6. Муж Э́мили – Крис. 7. Он рабо́тает в большо́й фи́рме в Нью-Йо́рке. 8. Да, он говори́т по-ру́сски. 9. Нет, он никогда́ не был в Росси́и. 10. Мо́жет быть, он бу́дет в Росси́и весно́й.
11. Роди́тели Э́мили живу́т в Калифо́рнии. 12. На фотогра́фии роди́тели му́жа. 13. Они́ живу́т в Конне́ктикуте.

Dialogue 2
ПЕ́РВОЕ ЗНАКО́МСТВО
FIRST INTRODUCTIONS

▶ 12A Dialogue 2 Russian Only (CD: 3, Track 18), 12B Dialogue 2 Russian and English (CD: 3, Track 19), 12C Dialogue 2 Role Play exercise (CD: 3, Track 20)

John Bradley, an American businessman, meets a Russian journalist, Natalia Petrova, in the airport in Moscow.

Джон:	Здра́вствуйте. Я Джон Брэ́дли. А вы?
John:	*Hello. I'm John Bradley. And you?*
Ната́лья:	Здра́вствуйте, господи́н Брэ́дли. О́чень прия́тно. Я Ната́лья Петро́ва.
Natalia:	*Hello, Mr. Bradley. Nice to meet you. I'm Natalia Petrova.*
Джон:	О́чень прия́тно, госпожа́ Петро́ва. Кто вы по профе́ссии?
John:	*Nice to meet you, Ms. Petrova. What do you do?*
Ната́лья:	Я журнали́стка. А кто вы по профе́ссии?
Natalia:	*I'm a journalist. And what do you do?*
Джон:	Я бизнесме́н. Вы ру́сская?
John:	*I'm a businessman. Are you Russian?*
Ната́лья:	Да, я ру́сская. Я из Москвы́. А отку́да вы?
Natalia:	*Yes, I am Russian. I'm from Moscow. Where are you from?*
Джон:	Я из Аме́рики.
John:	*I'm from America.*
Ната́лья:	Вот как? О́чень интере́сно! Я неда́вно была́ в Аме́рике.
Natalia:	*Oh, really? Very interesting. I was recently in America.*
Джон:	Где вы бы́ли в Аме́рике?
John:	*Where were you in America?*
Ната́лья:	Я была́ оди́н ме́сяц в Нью-Йо́рке и две неде́ли в Вашингто́не. Мне там о́чень понра́вилось.

Natalia:	I was in New York for a month and in Washington for two weeks. I liked it very much there.
Джон:	Я о́чень рад!
John:	I'm very glad!
Ната́лья:	Добро́ пожа́ловать в Росси́ю! Я наде́юсь, вам здесь то́же понра́вится.
Natalia:	Welcome to Russia! I hope you like it here, too.
Джон:	Большо́е спаси́бо! До свида́ния.
John:	Thank you very much! Good-bye!
Ната́лья:	Счастли́во!
Natalia:	So long! (lit., Happily!)

✎ Dialogue 2 Practice

Let's practice what you've learned in this dialogue.

1. Кто господи́н Брэ́дли по профе́ссии?

   _____

2. Кто госпожа́ Петро́ва по профе́ссии?

   _____

3. Госпожа́ Петро́ва америка́нка?

   _____

4. Отку́да господи́н Брэ́дли?

   _____

5. Ната́лья живёт в Аме́рике?

   _____

6. Где в Аме́рике была́ Ната́лья?

_____

7. Когда́ Ната́лья была́ в Аме́рике?

_____

8. В како́м америка́нском го́роде Ната́лья жила́ оди́н ме́сяц?

_____

9. В како́м амери́канском го́роде Ната́лья была́ две неде́ли?

_____

10. Ната́лье понра́вилось в Аме́рике?

_____

11. Кто говори́т: «Добро́ пожа́ловать?»

_____

12. Кто говори́т: «Большо́е спаси́бо?»

_____

ANSWER KEY

1. Господи́н Брэ́дли – бизнесме́н. 2. Госпожа́ Петро́ва – журнали́стка. 3. Нет, госпожа́ Петро́ва – ру́сская. 4. Господин Брэдли из Аме́рики. 5. Нет, Ната́лья живёт в Росси́и. 6. Наталья была́ в Нью-Йорке и в Вашингто́не. 7. Ната́лья неда́вно была́ в Аме́рике. 8. Ната́лья жила́ ме́сяц в Нью-Йорке. 9. Ната́лья жила́ две неде́ли в Вашингто́не. 10. Да, ей понра́вилось в Аме́рике. 11. Ната́лья говори́т: «Добро́ пожа́ловать!» 12. Джон говори́т: «Большо́е спаси́бо!»

🔊 Dialogue 3
В УНИВЕРСИТÉТЕ
AT THE UNIVERSITY

▶ 13A Dialogue 3 Russian Only (CD: 3, Track 21), 13B Dialogue 3 Russian and English (CD: 3, Track 22), 13C Dialogue 3 Role Play exercise (CD: 3, Track 23)

Sean, an American student, is visiting a Russian university and meeting a Russian student there, Olga.

Шон:	Извини́те, пожа́луйста, вы студе́нтка?
Sean:	*Excuse me please, are you a student?*
Óльга:	Да, я студе́нтка. Э́то мой университе́т.
Olga:	*Yes, I'm a student. This is my university.*
Шон:	Я то́же студе́нт.
Sean:	*I'm also a student.*
Óльга:	Отку́да вы?
Olga:	*Where are you from?*
Шон:	Я из Нью-Йо́рка. Я америка́нец.
Sean:	*I'm from New York. I'm an American.*
Óльга:	Пра́вда? А как вас зову́т?
Olga:	*Really? And what's your name?*
Шон:	Меня́ зову́т Шон. А как вас зову́т?
Sean:	*My name is Sean. And what is your name?*
Óльга:	Óчень прия́тно, Шон. Меня́ зову́т Óльга, или про́сто Óля. Дава́йте на "ты."
Olga:	*Nice to meet you, Sean. My name is Olga or simply Olya. Let's be informal.*
Шон:	Прия́тно познако́миться, Óля. Коне́чно, дава́й на "ты." Э́то твои друзья́ там?
Sean:	*Nice to meet you, Olya. Of course, let's be informal. Are those your friends over there?*

Essential Russian

Óльга:	Да, они́ то́же студе́нты. Пойдём, я тебя́ познако́млю.
Olga:	*Yes, they are students too. Let's go, I'll introduce you.*
Шон:	С удово́льствием! Пойдём.
Sean:	*Sure (lit., with pleasure). Let's go.*

✎ Dialogue 3 Practice

Let's see if you've understood everything. Listen to the dialogue as many times as you'd like, to check your answers.

1. Кто тако́й Шон?

   _____

2. Кто така́я О́льга?

   _____

3. Отку́да Шон?

   _____

4. Отку́да О́льга?

   _____

5. Чей э́то университе́т?

   _____

6. Кто пе́рвый говори́т: «Дава́йте на "ты"?»

   _____

7. Кто говори́т: «О́чень прия́тно?»

   _____

8. Кто говори́т: «Прия́тно познако́миться?»

_____

9. Кто ещё там?

_____

10. Кто дру́зья О́льги?

_____

11. Кто говори́т: «Пойдём, я тебя́ познако́млю?»

_____

12. Что говори́т Шон?

_____

ANSWER KEY
1. Шон – америка́нский студе́нт. 2. О́льга – ру́сская студе́нтка. 3. Шон из Нью-Йо́рка. 4. О́льга из э́того университе́та. 5. Э́то её университе́т. 6. О́льга пе́рвая говори́т: «Дава́йте на ты». 7. О́льга говори́т: «О́чень прия́тно». 8. Шон говори́т: «Прия́тно познако́миться». 9. Ещё там её друзья́. 10. Они́ то́же студе́нты. 11. О́льга говори́т: «Пойдём, я тебя познако́млю». 12. Шон говори́т: «С удово́льствием!»

Dialogue 4
ИДЁМ ЗАВТРАКАТЬ!
LET'S GO HAVE BREAKFAST!

▶ 14A Dialogue 4 Russian Only (CD: 3, Track 24), 14B Dialogue 4 Russian and English (CD: 3, Track 25), 14C Dialogue 4 Role Play exercise (CD: 3, Track 26)

An American tourist Kevin is meeting his Russian friend Vera on Nevsky Avenue in St. Petersburg in the morning. They are walking to a café to have breakfast.

Ке́вин:	Здра́вствуй, Ве́ра!
Kevin:	*Hello, Vera!*
Ве́ра:	Приве́т, Ке́вин!

Vera:	*Hello, Kevin!*
Ке́вин:	Как у тебя́ дела́?
Kevin:	*How are you doing?*
Ве́ра:	Спаси́бо, хорошо́. А как у тебя́?
Vera:	*Fine, thank you. And you?*
Ке́вин:	Всё отли́чно! Скажи́, пожа́луйста, ты уже́ за́втракала?
Kevin:	*Everything is great! Tell (me) please, have you already have breakfast?*
Ве́ра:	Нет ещё. А ты?
Vera:	*Not yet. And you?*
Ке́вин:	Я то́же ещё не за́втракал. Ты не зна́ешь, где здесь мо́жно хорошо́ поза́втракать?
Kevin:	*I also haven't. Do you (happen to) know where we could have a good breakfast?*
Ве́ра:	Пойдём в кни́жный магази́н о́коло метро́. Там на второ́м этаже́ есть отли́чное кафе́.
Vera:	*Let's go to the bookstore by the metro. They have an excellent café there on the second floor.*
Ке́вин:	А что там есть на за́втрак? Там есть фру́кты или мю́сли?
Kevin:	*What do they have for breakfast? Do they have (lit., are there) fruits and cereal?*
Ве́ра:	Да, коне́чно есть. Там есть ещё и блины́, и омле́т, и бутербро́ды.
Vera:	*Yes, of course (there are). They also have pancakes, omelets, and sandwiches.*
Ке́вин:	Отли́чно! Пойдём туда́. А на у́жин я хочу́ пойти́ в ру́сский рестора́н. Я люблю́ ру́сскую ку́хню!
Kevin:	*Great! Let's go there. And for dinner, I want (would like to) go to a Russian restaurant. I like Russian cuisine.*
Ве́ра:	Я зна́ю оди́н хоро́ший рестора́н в це́нтре. Там ру́сская ку́хня.
Vera:	*I know one good restaurant downtown. It has Russian cuisine.*

Кéвин:	Отлúчно! Спасúбо!
Kevin:	*Great! Thank you!*
Вéра:	Не за что. Ну, вот и кафé. Вон там, у окна есть свобóдный стóлик. Пойдём тудá.
Vera:	*Not at all. Well, here's the café. There's a free table over there by the window. Let's go there.*
Кéвин:	Пойдём. Ты что будешь пить, чай или кóфе?
Kevin:	*Let's (do it). What will drink, tea or coffee?*
Вéра:	Я бýду апельсúновый сок и капучúно. А ты?
Vera:	*I'll have orange juice and cappuccino. And you?*
Кéвин:	А я бýду зелёный чай с жасмúном. Прия́тного аппетúта!
Kevin:	*I'll have green tea with jasmine. Bon appétit!*

✎ Dialogue 4 Practice

А сейчáс, отвéтьте на вопрóсы. *And now, answer the questions.*

1. Где сейчáс Кéвин и Вéра?

   _____

2. Как делá у Кéвина?

   _____

3. Как делá у Вéры?

   _____

4. Кéвин зáвтракал сегóдня ýтром?

   _____

5. А Вéра ужé зáвтракала?

   _____

6. Где кни́жный магази́н?

_____

7. Где Ке́вин и Ве́ра бу́дут за́втракать?

_____

8. На како́м этаже́ кафе́?

_____

9. В кафе́ есть фру́кты и мю́сли?

_____

10. Где Ке́вин хо́чет у́жинать?

_____

11. Каку́ю ку́хню лю́бит Ке́вин?

_____

12. Что Ве́ра бу́дет пить на за́втрак?

_____

13. Что Ке́вин бу́дет пить на за́втрак?

_____

ANSWER KEY

1. Ке́вин и Ве́ра на Не́вском проспе́кте в Санкт-Петербу́рге. 2. У Ке́вина всё хорошо́.
3. У Ве́ры всё отли́чно. 4. Нет, Ке́вин ещё не за́втракал. 5. Нет, Вера ещё не за́втракала.
6. Кни́жный магази́н о́коло метро́. 7. Ке́вин и Ве́ра бу́дут за́втракать в кафе́ в кни́жном
магази́не. 8. Кафе́ на второ́м этаже́. 9. Да, в кафе́ есть фру́кты и мю́сли. 10. Ке́вин хо́чет
у́жинать в ру́сском рестора́не. 11. Ке́вин лю́бит ру́сскую ку́хню. 12. Ве́ра бу́дет пить
апельси́новый сок и капучи́но. 13. Ке́вин бу́дет пить зелёный чай с жасми́ном.

🔊 Dialogue 5
ПРОДУ́КТЫ ДЛЯ ВЕЧЕРИ́НКИ
FOOD FOR A PARTY

▶ 15A Dialogue 5 Russian Only (CD: 3, Track 27), 15B Dialogue 5 Russian and English (CD: 3, Track 28), 15C Dialogue 5 Role Play exercise (CD: 3, Track 29)

In this dialogue, an American exchange student Bill and his Russian roommate Anya are going to through a party. Now they are planning for it.

Билл:	Аня, ты по́мнишь, что в суббо́ту у нас до́ма бу́дет вечери́нка?
Bill:	*Anya, do you remember that we'll have a party on Saturday?*
Аня:	Да, коне́чно. Наве́рное, нам ну́жно пойти́ в магази́н и купи́ть что́-нибудь. Что нам ну́жно?
Anya:	*Yes, of course. We probably need to go to the store and buy something. What do we need?*
Билл:	Нам ну́жно купи́ть сыр, колбасу́, хлеб, оли́вки, сала́т, помидо́ры и фру́кты. Что́-нибудь ещё?
Bill:	*We need to buy cheese, sausage, bread, olives, salad, tomatoes, and fruit. Anything else?*
Аня:	Да, коне́чно. Ещё вино́, кра́сное и бе́лое, пи́во, сок и минера́льную во́ду. Всё это бу́дет в но́вом большо́м суперма́ркете.
Anya:	*Yes, of course. We also need wine, red and white, beer, juice, and mineral water. All these will be (available) in the big new supermarket.*
Билл:	Да́же алкого́ль?
Bill:	*Even alcohol?*
Аня:	Да, коне́чно. Там есть большо́й ви́нный отде́л.
Anya:	*Sure. They have a large wine/alcohol department there.*
Билл:	А во ско́лько у нас бу́дет вечери́нка?

Bill:	*What time is the party?*
Аня:	Го́сти приду́т в семь часо́в ве́чера.
Anya:	*Guests will come at seven p.m.*
Билл:	Э́то хорошо́. У нас днём бу́дет вре́мя всё подгото́вить.
Bill:	*That's good. We'll have time in the afternoon to prepare everything.*

✎ Dialogue 5 Practice

Мо́жете отве́тить на э́ти вопро́сы? *Can you answer these questions?*

1. Что бу́дет в суббо́ту?

   _____

2. Каки́е проду́кты им ну́жно купи́ть в магази́не?

   _____

3. Что ещё им ну́жно купи́ть в магази́не?

   _____

4. Како́е вино́ им ну́жно купи́ть?

   _____

5. Где они́ ку́пят все проду́кты?

   _____

6. Где они́ ку́пят вино́ и пи́во?

   _____

7. Что мо́жно купи́ть в ви́нном отде́ле?

   _____

8.   Во сколько будет вечеринка?

_____

9.   Что гости будут пить на вечеринке?

_____

10. Что гости будут есть на вечеринке?

_____

11. Где будет вечеринка?

_____

12. Когда у Билла и Ани будет время всё подготовить?

_____

ANSWER KEY

1. В субботу будет вечеринка. 2. Им нужно купить сыр, колбасу, хлеб, оливки, салат, помидоры и фрукты. 3. Ещё им нужно купить вино, пиво, сок и минеральную воду. 4. Им нужно купить красное и белое вино. 5. Они купят все продукты в большом новом супермаркете. 6. Они купят вино и пиво в винном отделе супермаркета. 7. В винном отделе можно купить алкоголь. 8. Вечеринка будет в семь часов вечера. 9. Гости будут пить вино, пиво, сок и минеральную воду. 10. Гости будут есть сыр, колбасу, хлеб, оливки, салат, помидоры и фрукты. 11. Вечеринка будет у Билла и Ани. 12. У Билла и Ани днём будет время всё подготовить.

The Cyrillic Alphabet: Handwriting

The first thing that often intimidates anyone learning Russian is the alphabet. Russian uses the Cyrillic alphabet, which is derived from the Greek alphabet, whereas English is written with the Latin alphabet. There are a few letters that are shared by both languages, and some letters may be familiar to you from basic mathematics and the names of college fraternities and sororities. As you use this book, you will quickly become familiar with the different letters and sounds, and soon you'll be able to recognize them instantly, reducing the intimidation factor.

Compare the handwritten to the printed Cyrillic letters in the chart below. Notice that print and handwritten letters differ at times.

PRINT	HANDWRITTEN	NAME
Аа	*А а*	ah
Бб	*Б б*	beh
Вв	*В в*	veh
Гг	*Г г*	geh
Дд	*Д д*	deh
Ее	*Е е*	yeh
Ёё	*Ё ё*	yoh
Жж	*Ж ж*	zheh
Зз	*З з*	zeh
Ии	*И и*	ee
Йй	*Й й*	ee kratkoye
Кк	*К к*	kah
Лл	*Л л*	ell
Мм	*М м*	em
Нн	*Н н*	en
Оо	*О о*	oh
Пп	*П п*	peh
Рр	*Р р*	err

PRINT	HANDWRITTEN	NAME
Сс	*Сс*	ess
Тт	*Тm*	teh
Уу	*Уу*	ooh
Фф	*Фф*	eff
Хх	*Хх*	khah
Цц	*Цц*	tseh
Чч	*Чч*	cheh
Шш	*Шш*	shah
Щщ	*Щщ*	shchah
Ыы	*ыы*	ih
Ъь	*ъь*	hard sign
Ьъ	*ьъ*	soft sign
Ээ	*Ээ*	eh
Юю	*Юю*	yoo
Яя	*Яя*	yah

Now let's look at some examples of handwritten Russian. Practice your own handwriting on the line below the handwritten words and phrases.

1. здравствуйте (*Hello [pl. or formal]*)

   здравствуйте

   _____

2. Очень приятно! (*Nice to meet you!*)

   Очень приятно!

   _____

3. Добро пожаловать! (*Welcome!*)

Добро пожаловать!

4. Как дела? (*How are you?*)

Как дела?

5. Хорошо. (*Well.*)

Хорошо.

6. Вы говорите по-русски? (*Do you speak Russian?*)

Вы говорите по-русски?

7. Пойдёмте! (*Let's go! [plural or formal]*)

Пойдёмте!

8. До свидания. (*Goodbye.*)

До свидания.

Pronunciation Guide

Russian pronunciation will be easy once you learn the rules of pronunciation and reading, which hold true with very few exceptions. It is just as easy to say *ah* as it is to say *oh*, or to say *vast* as it is to say *fast*. But if you pronounce *f* where it should be *v*, or *oh* where it should be *ah*, or *eh* where it should be *ee*, it would be difficult to understand you. Knowing these rules will help you to have a sound picture of the word you are learning and will help you to recognize it when it is spoken by native speakers; you want to understand as well as to speak!

1. Russian spelling is not phonetic. Spelling and sound don't always match up. Many native Russians think it does, but they are wrong!

2. Learn word units. Always try to pronounce pronouns, prepositions, and adjectives together with the words they modify. Note that all words that have more than one syllable are marked with an accent mark. This is done only for the sake of the student. Accent marks will not be found in reading material outside of textbooks, but for the sake of proper pronunciation, it is necessary to memorize the stress in each word.

3. Russian punctuation varies little from that of English in the use of the semicolon, colon, exclamation point, question mark, and period. However, the use of the comma is determined by concrete grammatical rules and generally does not, as in English, indicate a pause in speech or an inversion in word order. Usually, commas in Russian indicate a new clause whether principle or subordinate; inversions within one clause don't need commas.

4. Many letters represent several sounds. It is important to keep this in mind at the beginning of your study and to acquire the proper reading and pronunciation habits at the very start.

5. The Russian language has twenty consonant letters representing thirty-five consonant sounds, because fifteen of these twenty letters can represent either soft or hard (palatalized or nonpalatalized) sounds. Three are hard only; three

are soft only including one semi-vowel (or glide). There are ten vowels and one semi-vowel. We discuss palatalization in more detail in *Essential* Lesson 1 Take It Further 3. For now, consider the following.

6. Softness, or palatalization, of consonants is indicated by the vowels: е, ё, и, ю, я, and ь (soft sign). When a consonant is followed by one of these vowels, the consonant is palatalized—i.e., it is soft. In palatalization, the articulation of a consonant in its nonpalatalized form is altered in a specific way: the place and manner of articulation remain the same, but the middle part of the speaker's tongue moves up to the palate and to the front to produce palatalization. Palatalization in the Russian language has particular significance and should therefore be carefully studied, as the meaning of a word changes through palatalization.

1. VOWELS

Now that you've looked at the difference between Russian and English on a broad scale, let's get down to the specifics by looking at individual sounds, starting with Russian vowels.

LETTER	PRONUNCIATION	EXAMPLES
Аа	*when stressed, like a in father*	а́рмия (*army*), ла́мпа (*lamp*), ма́ло (*little*)
	when unstressed, like a in father, but shorter	команди́р (*commander*), каде́т (*cadet*)
	otherwise, like the a in sofa	каранда́ш (*pencil*), магази́н (*store*), аванга́рд (*avant-garde*)
Оо	*when stressed, like the o in gone or aw in saw*	он (*he*), до́брый (*kind*)

LETTER	PRONUNCIATION	EXAMPLES
	when unstressed, either in first place before the stressed syllable or used initially, like the o in sob	Борúс (*Boris*), онá (*she*), онó (*it*), отвечáть (*to answer*)
	otherwise, like the a in sofa	хорошó (*well*), плóхо (*badly*), молокó (*milk*)
Уу	*like the oo in food*	стул (*chair*), суп (*soup*), ýтро (*morning*), тудá (*there*), урóк (*lesson*), узнавáть (*to find out*), учúтель (*teacher*)
ы	*similar to the i in sit but more "throaty"*	ты (*you*), мы (*we*), вы (*pl,. you*), мы́ло (*soap*), малы́ (*short adj., small*), столы́ (*tables*), былá (*she was*)
Ээ	*like the e in echo*	э́то (*this*), э́ти (*these*), поэ́т (*poet*), этáп (*period, stage*)

The function of the vowels е, ё, и, ю, я, which are preceded by a glide (the sound similar to the final sound in the English word *may*), is the palatalization of the previous consonant, to which they lose the above-mentioned glide. However,

Essential Russian

when they follow a vowel or soft or hard signs, or when they appear initially, they are pronounced as in the alphabet—i.e., with the initial glide.

LETTER	PRONUNCIATION	EXAMPLES
Ее	*when stressed, like the ye in yet; it always palatalizes the preceding consonant, except the letters* ж, ц, *and* ш *(which are always hard)*	нет (*no*), Вéра (*Vera, faith*), сесть (*to sit down*)
	when unstressed, like the i in sit	всегдá (*always*), сестрá (*sister*), женá (*wife*)
	initially, or after another vowel, with the glide stressed, like ye in yet, or unstressed, like ye	ей (*to her*), её (*her*), поéздка (*trip*)
Ёё	*like the yo in yoke; always palatalizes the preceding consonant, except the letters* ж, ц, *and* ш *(which are always hard) and is always stressed*	мёд (*honey*), тётя (*aunt*), ёлка (*fir tree*), моё (*my*), ещё (*yet, still*)
Ии	*like ee in beet; always palatalizes the preceding consonant, except the letters* ж, ц, *and* ш *(which are always hard)*	сúла (*strength*), Лиза (*Liza*), никогдá (*never*), иногдá (*sometimes*)
	after the letters ж, ц, *and* ш, *like the Russian sound* ы	шúна (*tire*), жúть (*live*)

LETTER	PRONUNCIATION	EXAMPLES
Йй	*like the y in boy*	мой (*my*), пойти́ (*to go*), споко́йно (*quietly*), Нью-Йорк (*New York*)
Юю	*in the middle of a word, like oo in food; it always palatalizes the preceding consonant*	Лю́ба (*Lyuba*), люблю́ (*I love*), люби́ть (*to love*)
	when used initially, it retains its glide and is pronounced like you	ю́бка (*skirt*), юбиле́й (*jubilee, anniversary*)
Яя	*when stressed in the middle of the word, like ya in yacht; it always palatalizes the preceding consonant*	мя́со (*meat*), мая́к (*lighthouse*)
	when unstressed, it is pronounced either like the ee of beet or like the a of sofa if it is the last letter of a word; it always palatalizes the preceding consonant	тётя (*aunt*), де́сять (*ten*)
	when stressed, like the ya in yacht; when used initially, it retains its glide	я́блоко (*apple*), янва́рь (*January*)
	when unstressed, like the yi in yippy	язы́к (*language, tongue*)

2. HARD AND SOFT SIGNS

LETTER	PRONUNCIATION	EXAMPLES
ь	*the soft sign; it palatalizes the preceding consonant, allowing the following vowel to retain its glide, and indicates that the preceding consonant is soft when written at the end of a word*	пьéса (*play*), пья́ный (*drunk*), свинья́ (*pig*)
ъ	*the hard sign; it indicates that the preceding consonant remains hard and that the following vowel retains its glide*	объём (*volume*), объясня́ть (*explain*)

3. CONSONANTS

Russian consonants, like those in most languages, may be voiced or voiceless. The distinction between voiced and voiceless consonants is based on one aspect of otherwise identical articulation: in voiced consonants, the vocal cords are involved in articulation, while in voiceless consonants, they are not.

б в г д ж з	(*voiced*)	*b v g d zh z*
п ф к т ш с	(*voiceless*)	*p f k t sh s*

When two consonants are pronounced together in Russian, the first one becomes like the second one if it can.

всё, все, вчера́	в = *v becomes voiceless; it's pronounced as f*

сде́лать, сдать	с = s becomes voiced; it's pronounced as z

The preposition в (*in*) is pronounced as *f* before voiceless consonants. В шко́ле (*in school*) is pronounced f shkoh-leh.

Russian consonants can also be soft or hard, i.e., palatalized or nonpalatalized. Exceptions are the consonants ж, ш, and ц, which are always hard and ч, щ, and й (the glide), which are always soft.

These rules seem complicated, but it is much easier to learn them in the beginning and to start reading and speaking correctly than it is to try to correct erroneous pronunciation later on.

LETTER	PRONUNCIATION	EXAMPLES
Бб	*like b in bread*	брат (*brother*), бума́га (*paper*), бага́ж (*baggage*)
	palatalized	бе́лый (*white*), бино́кль (*binoculars*)
	at the end of a word or before a voiceless consonant, like the p in hip	ю́бка (*skirt*), зуб (*tooth*), хлеб (*bread*)
	voiceless palatalized	дробь (*buckshot*), зыбь (*ripple*)
Вв	*like the v in very*	ваш (*your*), вот (*here*), вода́ (*water*)
	palatalized	ве́ра (*faith*), конве́рт (*envelope*), весь (*all*)

Essential Russian

LETTER	PRONUNCIATION	EXAMPLES
	at the end of a word or before a voiceless consonant, like the f in half	Ки́ев (*Kiev*), в шко́ле (*in school*), вчера́ (*yesterday*), кров (*shelter*)
	voiceless palatalized	кровь (*blood*)
Гг	*like the g in good*	газе́та (*newspaper*), где (*where*), гармо́ния (*harmony*)
	palatalized	гита́ра (*guitar*), геоме́трия (*geometry*)
	before к, *like the Russian* к *or* х *(see below)*	легко́ (*lightly, easily*), мя́гко (*softly*)
	between е *and* о, *like the v in victor*	его́ (*his*), ничего́ (*nothing*), сего́дня (*today*)
	at the end of a word, voiceless, like the k in rock	рог (*horn*), четве́рг (*Thursday*)
Дд	*like the d in door*	дом (*house*), родно́й (*kindred*)
	palatalized	де́рево (*wood*), оди́н (*one*)
	at the end of a word or before a voiceless consonant, like the t in take	обе́д (*dinner*), подко́ва (*horseshoe*), по́дпись (*signature*)
	voiceless palatalized	грудь (*breast*)

LETTER	PRONUNCIATION	EXAMPLES
Жж	*like s in measure*	жар (*heat*), жена́ (*wife*), жить (*to live*), пожа́р (*fire*)
	at the end of a word or before a voiceless consonant, like the sh in shake	ло́жка (*spoon*), муж (*husband*)
	it always stays hard evern before "soft" vowels	живо́т (*abdomen*), Жора́ (*first name*)
Зз	*like the z in zebra*	зда́ние (*building*), знать (*to know*)
	palatalized	зелёный (*green*), зима́ (*winter*)
	at the end of a word or before a voiceless consonant, like the s in sit	ползти́ (*crawl*), воз (*cart*)
Кк	*like the k in kept*	кни́га (*book*), класс (*class*), каранда́ш (*pencil*)
	palatalized	ке́пка (*cap*), кероси́н (*kerosene*), Ки́ев (*Kiev*), кино́ (*movie*)
	before a voiced consonant, voiced, like the g in good	вокза́л (*railroad station*), экза́мен (*examination*), к бра́ту (*to the brother*)
Лл	*like the l in look*	ло́жка (*spoon*), ла́мпа (*lamp*), мел (*chalk*)

LETTER	PRONUNCIATION	EXAMPLES
	palatalized, a bit like the ll in million	любо́вь (*love*), лёгкий (*light*), мель (*shoal*), боль (*pain*)
Мм	*like the m in man*	ма́ма (*mama*), магни́т (*magnet*), дом (*house*), паро́м (*ferry*)
	palatalized	мя́со (*meat*), ми́на (*mine*)
Нн	*like the n in noon*	нос (*nose*), нож (*knife*), балко́н (*balcony*)
	palatalized	не́бо (*sky*), неде́ля (*week*), ня́ня (*nurse*), конь (*horse*)
Пп	*palatalized*	пе́рвый (*first*), письмо́ (*letter*), цепь (*chain*)
Рр	*like the r in root*	ру́сский (*Russian*), пара́д (*parade*), пода́рок (*gift*), рука́ (*hand*)
	palatalized	рис (*rice*), поря́док (*order*), дверь (*door*)
Сс	*like the s in see*	сон (*dream*), суп (*soup*), свет (*light*), мясо (*meat*), ма́сло (*butter*)
	palatalized	се́вер (*north*), село́ (*village*), весь (*all*)
	before a voiced consonant, voiced, like the z in zebra	сде́лать (*to do*), сгоре́ть (*to burn down*)

LETTER	PRONUNCIATION	EXAMPLES
Тт	*like the t in table*	табáк (*tobacco*), тот (*that*), стол (*table*), тогдá (*then*)
	palatalized	тень (*shade*), стенá (*wall*)
	before a voiced consonant, like the d in dark	отдáть (*to give away*), отгадáть (*to guess*)
Фф	*like the f in friend*	фáбрика (*factory*), Фрáнция (*France*), фарфóр (*porcelain*)
	palatalized	афúша (*poster*)
	before a voiced consonant, like the v in victor	афгáнец (*Afghan*)
Хх	*like the ch in loch*	тúхо (*quietly*), хорошó (*well*), тéхника (*technique*), блохá (*flea*)
	palatalized	хúна (*quinine*), хúмия (*chemistry*)
Цц	*like the ts in gets*	цветóк (*flower*), цепь (*chain*), цирк (*circus*), пациéнт (*patient*), пéрец (*pepper*)
Чч	*before a vowel, like the ch in church; it is always soft even after "hard" vowels*	чай (*tea*), час (*hour*), чáсто (*often*), чемодáн (*suitcase*)
	before a consonant, like the sh in shall	что (*what*), конéчно (*of course*)

Essential Russian

LETTER	PRONUNCIATION	EXAMPLES
Шш	*like the sh in shall*	шаг за ша́гом (*step after step*), ша́хматы (*chess*), ши́на (*tire*), шёлк (*silk*), шерсть (*wool*), ты говори́шь (*you speak (sing.)*)
Щщ	*like the shch in fresh cheese; it is always soft even after "hard" vowels*	щека́ (*cheek*), щётка (*brush*), по́мощь (*help*), посещение (*visit*), ща́вель (*sorrel*)

4. SPELLING RULES

All Russian endings fall under two general categories: hard and soft. Hard endings follow hard consonants and soft endings follow soft consonants to maintain vowel correspondence.

VOWELS IN HARD ENDINGS	VOWELS IN SOFT ENDINGS
а	я
о	ё
у	ю
ы	и
э	е

However, an additional complication interferes with this fairly straightforward system and overrides it. This complication is usually referred to as the spelling rule. The spelling rule concerns only eight consonants: four hushers (because they produce a hushing sound)—ж, ш, щ, ч; three gutturals (because they are pronounced in the back of your mouth)—г, к, х; and the letter ц.

All gutturals and all hushers must be followed by the letters: а, у, and и (and never by я, ю, ы)!

Ц is followed by an ы at the end of the word, but by an и in the middle.

All hushers and ц must be followed by either a stressed о or an unstressed е!

Memorize this spelling rule and always keep it in mind along with the above chart! They will take mystery out of the Russian endings and will reduce in half what you otherwise would have to memorize mechanically.

Keep in mind the following points:

- жо and жё, and цэ and це, are pronounced alike.
- цы and ци, шо and шё, and the letters ж, ц, and ш are always hard.
- чо and чё, що and щё, and the letters ч and щ are always soft.

Read these rules over and over again. Listen to the recordings several times. You have learned them not when you have read and understood the rules, but when you can remember and repeat the sounds and words correctly without looking at the book. Master these, and you will speak Russian well.

Five fundamental rules

1. Remember which syllable is stressed; all others will be reduced.

2. Remember that unstressed о is pronounced *ah* in prestressed positions including unstressed positions in the beginning of the word and as a very short sound ә (*schwa*) in all other unstressed positions.

3. Remember that when two consonants are next to each other, the first changes according to the second; all voiced consonants become voiceless at the end of the word (if they can).

4. Remember that unstressed e and я in prestressed syllables are pronounced *eeh*.

5. Remember that the letters e, ё, и, ю, я, and ь palatalize the preceding consonant, unless it has no palatalized counterpart.

6. Remember that the letters e, ё, ю and я lose their initial glide й after consonants, but retain it after vowels, the soft and hard signs (ь and ъ), and in the beginning of the word.

Grammar Summary

1. THE RUSSIAN ALPHABET

RUSSIAN LETTER	NAME
Аа	*ah*
Бб	*beh*
Вв	*veh*
Гг	*geh*
Дд	*deh*
Ее	*yeh*
Ёё	*yoh*
Жж	*zheh*
Зз	*zeh*
Ии	*ee*
Йй	*ee krátkoye*
Кк	*kah*
Лл	*el*
Мм	*em*
Нн	*en*
Оо	*oh, aw*
Пп	*peh*
Рр	*er*
Сс	*es*
Тт	*teh*
Уу	*oo*
Фф	*ef*
Хх	*khah*
Цц	*tseh*
Чч	*cheh*
Шш	*shah*
Щщ	*shchah*

RUSSIAN LETTER	NAME
ы	*i*
ь	*soft sign*
ъ	*hard sign*
Ээ	*eh*
Юю	*yoo*
Яя	*yah*

2. PRONUNCIATION

VOWELS

The letter a, when stressed, is pronounced like the English *ah*; when unstressed before a stressed syllable, a is pronounced *ah*, but shorter, and in most other positions is given a brief sound, the so called *shwa* sound /ə/ as in the English *but* or *fun*. Like in English, the Russian /ə/ (*shwa*) cannot be stressed.

The letter o, when stressed, is pronounced *oh* or *aw* as in *saw* (spoken with a rounded east coast accent) but it is not a diphthong, that is, it is never pronounced as a long *o* in the English *Oh!* or *Joe*; when unstressed in first place before the stressed syllable or used initially, o is pronounced *ah* (indistinguishable from a), and in all other positions it becomes a *shwa* /ə/ (just like an a).

The letter y is pronounced both stressed and unstressed like the English *oo* in *hook* or *loop*, except that the unstressed y is a bit shorter.

The letter ы doesn't have an exact English equivalent; it is somewhat similar to the *i* sound in *silly*.

The letter э is pronounced like the *eh* in *echo*.

Five vowels—е, ё, и, ю, and я—have a glide (the sound similar to the final sound in the English word *boy* and the Russian й) in front of them. The function of these vowels is the palatalization (softening) of the preceding consonant, to which they lose the above-mentioned glide. However, when they follow a vowel or a soft or hard sign, or when they appear in the initial position in a word, they are pronounced as in the alphabet, i.e., with the initial glide.

The letter и always palatalizes the preceding consonant and is pronounced like the *ee* in *beet*, except when it follows the letters ж, ц, and ш (which are never palatalized); then it is pronounced like the Russian sound ы.

The letter е always palatalizes the consonant that precedes it, except when the consonant is ж, ц, or ш. When stressed, it is pronounced like the *yeh* in *yet*; in unstressed positions it is pronounced like the *ee* in *beet*. In the beginning of a word, it is pronounced with the glide: when stressed, like *yeh*; unstressed, like *yeeh*.

The letter ё always palatalizes the preceding consonant, and is always stressed. It is pronounced *yoh* as in *yawn* (spoken with a rounded east coast accent).

The letter я always palatalizes the preceding consonant; when stressed, it is pronounced *yah,* and when unstressed, it is pronounced like a shortened *ee*. In the initial position, it retains its glide; when stressed, it is pronounced *yah*, and when unstressed, *ee* (after consonants) and *yeeh* (elsewhere).

The letter ю always palatalizes the preceding consonant. It is pronounced *yoo* everywhere exept after consonants where it loses its glide and becomes a "soft" *oo* (like the French *u* in *tu* or the German *ü* in *über*).

The letter ь is called the soft sign; it palatalizes the preceding consonant, allowing the following vowel to retain its glide.

The letter ъ is called the hard sign. It indicates that the preceding consonant remains hard and that the following vowel retains its glide.

The glide й is more a consonant than a vowel: it can never be stressed or form a syllable. It is pronounced like the final sound in *boy*.

CONSONANTS

As in many languages, most Russian consonants may be voiced or voiceless, and form several pairs.

	RUSSIAN	ENGLISH
voiced	б в г д ж з	*b v g d zh z*
voiceless	п ф к т ш с	*p f k t sh s*

When two consonants are pronounced together, they must both be either voiced or voiceless. In Russian, the second one always remains as it is, and the first one changes accordingly.

всё, все, вчерá	в (*v*) pronounced as *f*
сделать, сдать	с (*s*) pronounced as *z*

The preposition в (*in*) is pronounced *f* before a voiceless consonant in the beginning of the next word: В шкóле is pronounced *f shkoh-leh*. All consonants—except л, м, н, and р—lose their voicing and become voiceless at the end of a word.

All consonants—except ж, ц, ш, ч, щ, and й—can also be either hard or soft (i.e., nonpalatalized or palatalized). They become soft when followed by the letter ё, и, ю, я or ь. ж, ц, and ш are always hard and ч, щ, and й (if we consider it a consonant) are always soft. One more note on pronunciation: the letter г, when appearing between the vowels e/o and o in grammatical endings, is pronounced *v*, as in the word ничегó, никогó.

3. GENDER

All Russian nouns, pronouns, adjectives, ordinal numerals, as well as cardinal numerals one and two, and even verbs in the past tense have gender: masculine, feminine, or neuter. There is no gender distinction in the plural.

	MASCULINE	FEMININE	NEUTER	PLURAL
Noun, pronoun, past tense verb endings	hard consonant, ь	а/я	о/е	а/я, ы/и
Adjective, ordinal numeral, participle ending	ой/ый/ий	ая/яя	ое/ее	ые/ие

Note: Pronouns, adjectives, and ordinal numerals always agree in gender and number with the nouns they modify.

4. CASES

a. With few exceptions, all nouns, pronouns, and adjectives decline, i.e. change form depending on their function in a sentence. Each declension has six cases.

Nominative	Кто? Что	*Who? What?*
Genitive	Кого? Чего? От кого? От чего? У кого? У чего? Без кого? Без чего?	*Whom? What?* *From whom? From what?* *At or by whom/what?* *Without whom/what?*
Dative	Кому? Чему? К кому? К чему?	*To whom? To what?* *Toward whom/what?*

Accusative	Кого́? Что? Куда́?	Whom? What? Where (direction toward)?
Instrumental	Кем? Чем? С кем? С чем?	By whom? By what? With whom? With what?
Prepositional or Locative	О ком? О чём? В ком? В чём? Где?	About whom/what? In whom? In what? Where (location)?

b. Overall characteristics of the cases and most used prepositions:

1. The nominative case is used for the subject of the sentence.

2. The genitive case is the case of possession and negation. It is also used with many prepositions, the most common of which are:

без	without
для	for
до	up to
из	out of
о́коло	near, next to
от	from
по́сле	after
у	at or by

3. The dative case is used in the meaning of to whom/what. Prepositions used with the dative case are:

к	toward
по	along

4. The accusative is the direct object case. It is also used after prepositions denoting direction:

в	*to, into*
за	*behind (direction), for, instead of*
на	*to, into, on (direction)*

5. The instrumental case indicates the manner of action or instrument with which the action is performed; the instrumental of means is used without prepositions. Prepositions used with the instrumental case include:

с	*with (together with, accompaniment)*
мéжду	*between*
пéред	*in front of*
над	*over*
под	*under (location)*
за	*behind (location)*

6. The prepositional or locative case indicates location and is also used when speaking about something or someone. This is the only case which cannot be used without prepositions. The prepositions most frequently used with this case are:

в	*in, at*
на	*on, at*
о/об	*about*
при	*in the presence of, under (the reign of)*

5. DECLENSION OF NOUNS

MASCULINE SINGULAR

	Hard: Animate	Hard: Inanimate	Soft: Animate	Soft: Inanimate
	student	*question*	*inhabitant*	*shed*
Nom.	студе́нт	вопро́с	жи́тель	сара́й
Gen.	студе́нт-а	вопро́с-а	жи́тел-я	сара́-я
Dat.	студе́нт-у	вопро́с-у	жи́тел-ю	сара́-ю
Acc.	студе́нт-а	вопро́с	жи́тел-я	сара́й
Inst.	студе́нт-ом	вопро́с-ом	жи́тел-ем	сара́-ем
Prep.	о студе́нт-е	о вопро́с-е	о жи́тел-е	о сара́-е

MASCULINE PLURAL

Nom.	студе́нт-ы	вопро́с-ы	жи́тел-и	сара́-и
Gen.	студе́нт-ов	вопро́с-ов	жи́тел-ей	сара́-ев
Dat.	студе́нт-ам	вопро́с-ам	жи́тел-ям	сара́-ям
Acc.	студе́нт-ов	вопро́с-ы	жи́тел-ей	сара́-и
Inst.	студе́нт-ами	вопро́с-ами	жи́тел-ями	сара́-ями
Prep.	о студе́нт-ах	о вопро́с-ах	о жи́тел-ях	о сара́-ях

Notice that the accusative case of animate masculine nouns (and all animate plural nouns) is the same as the genitive, while the accusative of inanimate masculine nouns is the same as the nominative.

FEMININE SINGULAR

	Hard	Soft	
	room	*earth*	*family*
Nom.	ко́мната	земля́	семья́
Gen.	ко́мнат-ы	земл-и́	семь-и́
Dat.	ко́мнат-е	земл-е́	семь-е́
Acc.	ко́мнат-у	зе́мл-ю	семь-ю́
Inst.	ко́мнат-ой(ою)	земл-ёй(ёю)	семь-ёй(ёю)

FEMININE SINGULAR			
	Hard	Soft	
	room	*earth*	*family*
Prep.	о ко́мнат-е	о земл-е́	о семь-е́

FEMININE PLURAL			
Nom.	ко́мнат-ы	зе́мл-ии	семь-и́
Gen.	ко́мнат	земе́л-ь	сем-е́й
Dat.	ко́мнат-ам	зе́мл-ям	се́мь-ям
Acc.	ко́мнат-ы	зе́мл-ии	се́мь-и́
Inst.	ко́мнат-ами	зе́мл-ями	се́мь-ями
Prep.	о ко́мнат-ах	о зе́мл-ях	о се́мь-ях

NEUTER SINGULAR			
	Hard	Soft	
	window	*sea*	*wish*
Nom.	окно́	мо́ре	жела́ние
Gen.	окн-а́	мо́р-я	жела́н-ия
Dat.	окн-у́	мо́р-ю	жела́н-ию
Acc.	окн-о́	мо́р-е	жела́н-ие
Inst.	окн-о́м	мо́р-ем	жела́н-ием
Prep.	об окн-е	о мо́р-е	о жела́н-ии

NEUTER PLURAL			
Nom.	о́кн-а	мор-я́	жела́н-ия
Gen.	о́к-оон	мор-е́й	жела́н-ий
Dat.	о́кн-ам	мор-я́м	жела́н-иям
Acc.	о́кн-а	мор-я́	жела́н-ия
Inst.	о́кн-ами	мор-я́ми	жела́н-иями
Prep.	об о́кн-ах	о мор-я́х	о жела́н-иях

*Note: The variants (ою), (ёю), and (ёю) in the instrumental case for feminine singular nouns are poetic, dialectal, or folksy. Also б is added to the preposition о (as in the prepositional case of hard neuter singular nouns) before vowels (excluding the vowels е, ё, я, and ю, which start with the glide й).

SOME IRREGULAR DECLENSIONS

SINGULAR	Masculine	Feminine		Neuter
	road	*mother*	*daughter*	*name*
Nom.	путь	мать	дочь	и́мя
Gen.	пут-и́	ма́т-ери	до́ч-ери	и́м-ени
Dat.	пут-и́	ма́т-ери	до́ч-ери	и́м-ени
Acc.	путь	мать	дочь	и́мя
Inst.	пут-ём	ма́т-ерью	до́ч-ерью	и́м-енем
Prep.	о пут-и́	о ма́т-ери	о до́ч-ери	об и́м-ени

PLURAL					
Nom.	пут-и́	ма́т-ери	до́ч-ери	им-ена́	де́т-и
Gen.	пут-е́й	мат-ере́й	доч-ере́й	им-ён	дет-е́й
Dat.	пут-я́м	мат-еря́м	доч-еря́м	им-ена́м	де́т-ям
Acc.	пут-и́	мат-ере́й	доч-ере́й*	им-ена́	дет-е́й*
Inst.	пут-я́ми	мат-еря́ми	доч-еря́ми	им-ена́ми	дет-ьми́
Prep.	о пут-я́х	о мат-еря́х	о доч-еря́х	об им-ена́х	о де́т-ях

*Note: Since there is no gender distinction in the plural, the accusative plural of all animate nouns is the same as the genitive plural.

6. DECLENSION OF ADJECTIVES

SINGULAR						
	Masc.	Fem.	Neut.	Masc.	Fem.	Neut.
	ый	ая	ое	ой	ая	ое
Nom.	но́вый	но́вая	но́вое	сухо́й	суха́я	сухо́е
Gen.	но́в-ого	но́в-ой	но́в-ого	сух-о́го	сух-о́й	сух-о́го
Dat.	но́в-ому	но́в-ой	но́в-ому	сух-о́му	сух-о́й	сух-о́му
Acc.	*same as nom. or gen.*	но́в-ую	но́в-ое	*same as nom. or gen.*	сух-у́ю	сух-о́е
Inst.	но́в-ым	но́в-ой(-ою)	но́в-ым	сух-и́м	сух-о́й(-ою)	сух-и́м
Prep.	о но́в-ом	о но́в-ой	о но́в-ом	о сух-о́м	о сух-о́й	о сух-о́м

PLURAL		
Nom.	но́в-ые	сух-и́е
Gen.	но́в-ых	сух-и́х
Dat.	но́в-ым	сух-и́м
Acc.	*same as nom. or gen.*	*same as nom. or gen.*
Inst.	но́в-ыми	сух-и́ми
Prep.	о но́в-ых	о сух-и́х

	SINGULAR			PLURAL
	Masc.	Fem.	Neut.	
NOM.	си́н-ий	си́н-яя	си́н-ее	си́н-ие
Gen.	си́н-его	си́н-ей	си́н-его	си́н-их
Dat.	си́н-ему	си́н-ей	си́н-ему	си́н-им
Acc.	*same as nom. or gen.*	си́н-юю	си́н-ее	*same as nom. or gen.*
Inst.	си́н-им	си́н-ей(-ею)	си́н-им	си́н-ими
Prep.	о си́н-ем	о си́н-ей	о си́н-ем	о си́н-их

7. DECLENSION OF PRONOUNS

Below are the personal pronouns in their various forms.

| | SINGULAR | | | | |
| | 1st person | 2nd person | 3rd person | | |
			MASC.	NEUT.	FEM.
Nom.	я	ты	он	оно́	она́
Gen.	меня́	тебя́	его́	его́	её
Dat.	мне	тебе	ему́	ему́	ей
Acc.	меня́	тебя́	его́	его́	её
Instr.	мной(-о́ю)	тобо́й(-о́ю)	им	им	ей (е́ю)
Prep.	обо мне	о тебе	о нём	о нём	о ней

| | PLURAL | | | REFLEXIVE |
	1st person	2nd person	3rd person	Reflexive pronoun (*sing. or pl.*)
Nom.	мы	вы	они́	—
Gen.	нас	вас	их	себя́
Dat.	нам	вам	им	себе
Acc.	нас	вас	их	себя́
Instr.	на́ми	ва́ми	и́ми	собо́й(-о́ю)
Prep.	о нас	о вас	о них	о себе

The various forms of *my* are shown below.

| | SINGULAR | | | PLURAL |
	Masc.	Fem.	Neut.	All genders
Nom.	мой	моя́	моё	мои́
Gen.	моего́	моей	моего́	мои́х
Dat.	моему́	моей	моему́	мои́м

	SINGULAR			PLURAL
	Masc.	Fem.	Neut.	All genders
Acc.	same as nom. or gen.	мою	моё	same as nom. or gen.
Inst.	мои́м	мое́й(-ею)	мои́м	мои́ми
Prep.	о мое́м	о мое́й	о мое́м	о мои́х

Твой (*your, sg.*), свой (*the subject's own*) are declined in the same way.

For the third-person possessive, the genitive case of the personal pronouns is used. It always agrees with the gender and number of the possessor.

NOMINATIVE	GENITIVE	ENGLISH
он	его́	*his*
она́	её	*her*
оно́	его́	*its*
они́	их	*their*

The various forms of *our* are shown below.

	SINGULAR			PLURAL
	Masc.	Fem.	Neut.	All genders
Nom.	наш	на́ша	на́ше	на́ши
Gen.	на́ш-его	на́ш-ей	на́ш-его	на́ш-их
Dat.	на́ш-ему	на́ш-ей	на́ш-ему	на́ш-им
Acc.	same as nom. or gen.	на́ш-у	на́ше	same as nom. or gen.
Inst.	на́ш-им	на́ш-ей(-ею)	на́ш-им	на́ш-ими
Prep.	о на́ш-ем	о на́ш-ей	о на́ш-ем	о на́ш-их

Ваш (*pl.* or *form., your*) is declined in the same way.

All is shown in its various forms below.

	SINGULAR			PLURAL
	Masc.	Fem.	Neut.	All genders
Nom.	весь	вся	всё	все
Gen.	вс-его́	вс-ей	вс-его́	вс-ех
Dat.	вс-ему́	вс-ей	вс-ему́	вс-ем
Acc.	same as nom. or gen.	вс-ю	всё	same as nom. or gen.
Inst.	вс-ем	вс-ей(-ею)	вс-ем	вс-еми
Prep.	обо вс-ём	обо вс-ей	обо вс-ём	обо вс-ех

The forms of the demonstratives *this/these* are shown below.

	SINGULAR			PLURAL
	Masc.	Fem.	Neut.	All genders
Nom.	э́тот	э́та	э́то	э́ти
Gen.	э́т-ого	э́т-ой	э́т-ого	э́т-их
Dat.	э́т-ому	э́т-ой	э́т-ому	э́т-им
Acc.	same as nom. or gen.	э́т-у	э́то	same as nom. or gen.
Inst.	э́т-им	э́т-ой	э́т-им	э́т-ими
Prep.	об э́т-ом	об э́т-ой	об э́т-ом	об э́т-их

The forms of the demonstratives *that/those* are shown below.

	SINGULAR			PLURAL
	Masc.	Fem.	Neut.	All genders
Nom.	тот	та	то	те
Gen.	т-ого́	т-ой	т-ого́	т-ех
Dat.	т-ому́	т-ой	т-ому́	т-ем

	SINGULAR			PLURAL
	Masc.	Fem.	Neut.	All genders
Acc.	same as nom. or gen.	т-у	т-о	same as nom. or gen.
Inst.	т-ем	т-ой	т-ем	т-еми
Prep.	о т-ом	о т-ой	о т-ом	о т-ех

The forms of *oneself/themselves* are shown below.

	SINGULAR			PLURAL
	Masc.	Fem.	Neut.	All genders
Nom.	сам	сама́	само́	са́ми
Gen.	сам-ого́	сам-о́й	сам-ого́	сам-и́х
Dat.	сам-ому́	сам-о́й	сам-ому́	сам-и́м
Acc.	same as nom. or gen.	сам-у́	сам-о	same as nom. or gen.
Inst.	сам-и́м	сам-о́й	сам-и́м	сам-и́ми
Prep.	о сам-о́м	о сам-о́й	о сам-о́м	о сам-и́х

The forms of *whose* are shown below.

	SINGULAR			PLURAL
	Masc.	Fem.	Neut.	All genders
Nom.	чей	чья	чьё	чьи
Gen.	чьего́	чьей	чьего́	чьих
Dat.	чьему́	чьей	чьему́	чьим
Acc.	same as nom. or gen.	чью	чьё	same as nom. or gen.
Inst.	чьим	чьей	чьим	чьи́ми
Prep.	о чьём	о чьей	о чьём	о чьих

8. THE COMPARATIVE OF ADJECTIVES

To form most comparatives of adjectives, drop the gender ending and add –ее for all genders and the plural. The adjective does not decline in the comparative.

краси́вый	*pretty*
краси́в-ее	*prettier*
тёплый	*warm*
тепл-е́е	*warmer*
весёлый	*merry*
весел-е́е	*merrier*

Comparative forms with one –е in the ending:

хоро́ший	*good*
лу́чше	*better*
большо́й	*big*
бо́льше	*bigger*
ма́ленький	*small*
ме́ньше	*smaller*
широ́кий	*wide*
ши́ре	*wider*
у́зкий	*narrow*
у́же	*narrower*
плохо́й	*bad*
ху́же	*worse*
высо́кий	*tall, high*
вы́ше	*taller, higher*
ти́хий	*quiet*
ти́ше	*quieter*
дорого́й	*dear, expensive*

доро́же	*dearer, more expensive*
просто́й	*simple*
про́ще	*simpler*
то́лстый	*fat, thick*
то́лще	*fatter, thicker*

9. THE SUPERLATIVE OF ADJECTIVES

The superlative of adjectives has two forms. The simpler form—the one we will discuss here—makes use of the word са́мый, са́мая, са́мое, са́мые (*the most*).

са́мый большо́й	*the biggest*
са́мая краси́вая	*the prettiest*
са́мый у́мный	*the most clever*

The word са́мый declines with the adjective:

в са́мом большо́м доме
in the largest house

Он пришёл с са́мой краси́вой женщиной.
He came with the prettiest woman.

10. CASES USED WITH CARDINAL NUMBERS ОДИ́Н (*M.*), ОДНА́ (*F.*), ОДНО́ (*N.*), ОДНИ́ (*PL.*) AND ДВА (*M.*), ДВЕ (*F.*), ДВА (*N.*).

A. When the number is used in the nominative case or accusative inanimate:

after оди́н, одна́, одно́—use the nominative singular;
after одни́—use the nominative plural;
after два, две, три, четы́ре—use the genitive singular;
after пять, шесть, семь, etc.—use the genitive plural.

B. When the number is compound, the case of the noun depends on the last digit (excluding the zero):

двáдцать одúн карандáш (*nominative singular*)
twenty-one pencils

двáдцать два карандашá (*genitive singular*)
twenty-two pencils

двáдцать пять карандашéй (*genitive plural*)
twenty-five pencils

11. DECLENSION OF CARDINAL NUMERALS

All cardinal numerals decline, agreeing in case with the noun they modify (with the exception of the nominative and the accusative inanimate cases, discussed above).

Я остáлся без однóй копéйки. (*genitive singular*)
I was left without one kopeck.

Он был там одúн мéсяц без двух дней. (*genitive plural*)
He was there one month less two days.

Мы пришлú к пятú часáм. (*dative plural*)
We arrived by five o'clock.

Онú говорят о семú кнúгах. (*prepositional plural*)
They are talking about seven books.

Declension of *One/Only*

	SINGULAR			PLURAL
	Masc.	Fem.	Neut.	All genders
Nom.	оди́н	одна́	одно́	одни́
Gen.	одного́	одно́й	одного́	одни́х
Dat.	одному́	одно́й	одному́	одни́м
Acc.	same as nom. or gen.	одну́	одно́	same as nom. or gen.
Inst.	одни́м	одно́й(-о́ю)	одни́м	одни́ми
Prep.	об одно́м	об одно́й	об одно́м	об одних

Declension of other numerals

	TWO	*THREE*	*FOUR*	*FIVE*
Nom.	два/две	три	четы́ре	пять
Gen.	двух	трёх	четырёх	пяти́
Dat.	двум	трём	четырём	пяти́
Acc.	same as nom. or gen.	same as nom. or gen.	same as nom. or gen.	пять
Inst.	двумя́	тремя́	четырьмя́	пятью́
Prep.	о двух	о трёх	о четырёх	о пяти́

Note: All numbers from 6 to 20 follow the same declension pattern as 5.

The numerals 40 (со́рок), 90 (девяно́сто), and 100 (сто) end in –a in all cases except for the nominative: сорока́, девяно́ста, and ста.

12. ORDINAL NUMERALS

All ordinal numerals are like adjectives, and decline in the same way as adjectives.

MASC.	FEM.	NEUT.	PLURAL (ALL GENDERS)
пе́рвый	пе́рвая	пе́рвое	пе́рвые
второ́й	втора́я	второ́е	вторы́е

When they are compound, only the last digit changes its form, and only that digit is declined.

двадца́тый век	*twentieth century*
Э́то бы́ло три́дцать пе́рвого декабря́.	*That was on December 31.*
тре́тий раз	*third time*
Втора́я мирова́я война́ зако́нчилась в ты́сяча девятьсо́т со́рок пя́том году́.	*World War II ended in 1945 (lit., one thousand, nine hundred, forty-fifth year).*
в пя́том году́ (*prep., sing.*)	*in the fifth year*

13. DOUBLE NEGATIVES

With negative ни–words such as:

ничего́	*nothing*
никто́	*nobody*
никогда́	*never*
никуда́	*nowhere*

a second negative не must be used before the verb:

Я ничего́	не	хочу́, зна́ю
I nothing	*not (don't)*	*want, know*
Никто́	не	ви́дит, говори́т
Nobody	*not (don't)*	*see, speak*

Он никогда́	не	был в Москве́
He never	*not (don't)*	*was in Moscow*
Мы никогда́	не	говори́м по-ру́сски
We never	*not (don't)*	*speak Russian*

14. VERBS

Regular Russian verbs have two conjugation types, Conjugation I and Conjugation II. Only three types of verbal stems belong to Conjugation II—e–types (e.g., ви́деть), и–types (e.g., говори́ть), and а2–types (e.g., слы́шать). All other regular verbs belong to Conjugation Type I (e.g., рабо́тать, жить, etc.). There are also irregular verbs (e.g., есть, хоте́ть). In addition, all Russian verbs are either imperfective or perfective.

A. Typical conjugations of imperfective verbs

First conjugation

ЧИТА́ТЬ *TO READ*	
Present tense:	я чита́ю ты чита́ешь он чита́ет мы чита́ем вы чита́ете они́ чита́ют
Past tense:	чита́л (*m.*) чита́ла (*f.*) чита́ло (*n.*) чита́ли (*pl.*)

ЧИТА́ТЬ *TO READ*	
Future tense:	я бу́ду чита́ть
	ты бу́дешь чита́ть
	он бу́дет чита́ть
	мы бу́дем чита́ть
	вы бу́дете чита́ть
	они́ бу́дут чита́ть
Imperative:	чита́й
	чита́йте

Participles

ACTIVE	
Present tense:	чита́ющий
Past tense:	чита́вший

PASSIVE	
Present tense:	чита́емый

GERUND	
Imperfective gerund:	чита́я

Second conjugation

ГОВОРИ́ТЬ *TO SPEAK*	
Present tense:	я говорю́
	ты говори́шь
	он говори́т
	мы говори́м
	вы говори́те
	они́ говоря́т

ГОВОРИ́ТЬ *TO SPEAK*	
Past tense:	говори́л (*m.*) говори́ла (*f.*) говори́ло (*n.*) говори́ли (*pl.*)
Future tense:	я бу́ду говори́ть ты бу́дешь говори́ть он бу́дет говори́ть мы бу́дем говори́ть вы бу́дете говори́ть они́ бу́дут говори́ть
Imperative:	говори́ говори́те

PARTICIPLES	
Present tense:	говоря́щий
Past tense:	говори́вший

GERUND	
Imperfective gerund:	говоря́

B. Mixed conjugation

PRESENT TENSE	
ХОТЕ́ТЬ *TO WANT*	
я хочу́	мы хоти́м
ты хо́чешь	вы хоти́те
он хо́чет	они́ хотя́т

Note: This verb in the singular has first conjugation endings with the т changing to ч (т/ч mutation). In the plural it has second conjugation endings. The past tense is regular.

C. Reflexive verbs

Verbs ending with –ся or –сь are reflexive. These verbs follow the general form of conjugation, retaining the endings –ся after consonants and –сь after vowels.

ЗАНИМА́ТЬСЯ *TO STUDY*	
я занима́юсь	мы занима́емся
ты занима́ешься	вы занима́етесь
он занима́ется	они́ занима́ются

D. The verb быть (*to be*)

The verb быть (*to be*) is usually omitted in the present tense, but is used in the past tense:

был (*m.*)
была́ (*f.*)
бы́ло (*n.*)
бы́ли (*pl.*)

and in the future tense:

я бу́ду	мы бу́дем
ты бу́дешь	вы бу́дете
он бу́дет	они́ бу́дут

It is also used as an auxiliary verb in the imperfective future tense.

E. Conjugations of other verbs in the present tense

БРАТЬ (NON-SYLLABIC A–TYPE, CONJUGATION I) *TO TAKE*	
я беру́	мы берём
ты берёшь	вы берёте

БРАТЬ (NON-SYLLABIC A–TYPE, CONJUGATION I)
TO TAKE

он берёт	они́ беру́т

ВЕСТИ́ (Д–TYPE, CONJUGATION I)
TO LEAD

я веду́	мы ведём
ты ведёшь	вы ведёте
он ведёт	они́ веду́т

ЖИТЬ (В–TYPE, CONJUGATION I)
TO LIVE

я живу́	мы живём
ты живёшь	вы живёте
он живёт	они́ живу́т

ЗВАТЬ (NON-SYLLABIC A–TYPE, CONJUGATION I)
TO CALL

я зову́	мы зовём
ты зовёшь	вы зовёте
он зовёт	они́ зову́т

НЕСТИ́ (С–TYPE, CONJUGATION I)
TO CARRY

я несу́	мы несём
ты несёшь	вы несёте
он несёт	они́ несу́т

ДАВА́ТЬ (АВАЙ–TYPE, CONJUGATION I)
TO GIVE

я даю́	мы даём
ты даёшь	вы даёте
он даёт	они́ даю́т

Essential Russian

F. Conjugations of irregular perfective verbs (perfective future)

ДАТЬ (IRREGULAR) TO GIVE	
я дам	мы дади́м
ты дашь	вы дади́те
он даст	они́ даду́т

СЕСТЬ (И–TYPE, CONJUGATION II) TO SIT DOWN	
я ся́ду	мы ся́дем
ты ся́дешь	вы ся́дете
он ся́дет	они́ ся́дут

G. Perfective and imperfective aspects of Russian verbs

Russian verbs are either perfective or imperfective. Imperfective verbs express continuous actions, durations, or single actions taken out of immediate contexts, so called "statements of fact." They have three tenses—past, present, and future. Perfective verbs indicate complete and completed singular actions, changes of state relative to the existing context, and multiple actions in quick succession; all perfective verbs presuppose the interlocutor's awareness of their context. They have only two tenses—past and future.

Some perfective verbs are formed by adding the prefixes с–, на–, вы–, в–, по–, etc. to imperfective verbs; some others add suffixes such as –и– or –ну–. When an imperfective verb is turned into a perfective one, its meaning changes dramatically so it becomes a different verb.

IMPERFECTIVE	PERFECTIVE
писа́ть	написать
to write	to write down, to complete a written assignment

IMPERFECTIVE	PERFECTIVE
	переписа́ть *to copy, to re-write*

When you need to use the new prefixed verb переписа́ть (*to copy, to re-write*) in the imperfective aspect without losing the meaning of the prefix (e.g., if you *copy* something every day), you form a so-called "secondary imperfective form" by adding new imperfective suffixes to the perfective (prefixed) stem. The most common secondary imperfective suffix is –ыва–, but suffixes –ва– or –a– are also possible.

IMPERFECTIVE	PERFECTIVE	IMPERFECTIVE
писа́ть *to write*	переписа́ть *to copy*	перепи́сывать
чита́ть *to read*	прочита́ть *to finish reading or to read through* перечита́ть *to read over*	прочи́тывать перечи́тывать
знать *to know*	узна́ть *to find out or to recognize*	узнава́ть
дава́ть *to give*	дать отда́ть *to give out or away* переда́ть *to pass* зада́ть *to assign* сдать *to deal cards*	отдава́ть передава́ть задава́ть сдава́ть

Some perfective verbs have different roots.

IMPERFECTIVE	PERFECTIVE
брать *to take*	взять *to take*
сади́ться *to sit*	сесть *to sit*
говори́ть *to speak*	сказа́ть *to say*

Prefixes can be added to either говори́ть or сказа́ть, and each addition makes a new verb, e.g.:

заговори́ть	*to begin talking*
заказа́ть	*to order something*
отговори́ть (отгова́ривать)	*to talk someone out of something*
рассказа́ть	*to tell a story*

The past tense of the perfective verb is formed in the same way as the past tense of the imperfective verb.

H. Future tense

The future tense has two forms: imperfective future and perfective future. As has already been pointed out, the imperfective future is formed by using the auxiliary verb быть with the infinitive of the imperfective verb.

я бу́ду	говори́ть, чита́ть, рабо́тать, etc.	*I will*	*speak, read, work, etc.*
ты бу́дешь		*you will*	
он бу́дет		*he will*	
мы бу́дем		*we will*	
вы бу́дете		*you will*	

они бу́дут		they will	

The perfective future is formed without the use of the auxiliary verb быть. Since perfective verbs don't have the present tense, their present tense endings signify future. You can tell the difference between present and future by looking at the stem, not the endings.

PRESENT		PERFECTIVE FUTURE	
я пишу́	I write	я напишу́	I will write
ты говори́шь	you speak	ты ска́жешь	you will say
мы чита́ем	we read	мы прочита́ем	we will read (it)
вы смо́трите	you look	вы посмо́трите	you will look
они е́дут	they go (by vehicle)	они прие́дут	they will come (by vehicle)

Note: The perfective verb is conjugated in the same way as the imperfective verb.

I. Verbs of motion

Verbs of motion have many variations of meaning. A different verb is used to express movement by vehicle than the one used to express movement on foot.

Each of these verbs (i.e., indicating movement on foot or movement by vehicle) has two forms: one describes a continuing or background action in one direction (unidirectional verb of motion), and the other, a single action in the past or a repeated/general action (multidirectional verb of motion). All of these forms are imperfective. The perfective is formed by adding a prefix to a unidirectional verb. But bear in mind that the addition of the prefix changes the meaning of the verb.

The same prefix (with the exception of the prefix по–) added to multidirectional verbs of motion forms the imperfective of a new verb.

IMPERFECTIVE	MULTIDIRECTIONAL		UNIDIRECTIONAL	PERFECTIVE
	ходи́ть	*to go on foot*	идти́	
	е́здить	*to go by vehicle*	е́хать	
выходи́ть		*to exit on foot*		вы́йти
выезжа́ть		*to drive out*		вы́ехать
приходи́ть		*to come on foot/arrive*		прийти́
приезжа́ть		*to come by vehicle/ arrive*		прие́хать
заходить		*to drop in/ visit on foot*		зайти́
заезжа́ть		*to drop in/ visit by vehicle*		зае́хать
	носи́ть	*to carry on foot*	нести́	
	вози́ть	*to carry by vehicle*	везти́	
приноси́ть		*to bring on foot*		принести́
привози́ть		*to bring by vehicle*		привезти́

ИДТИ
TO WALK (UNIDIRECTIONAL)

PRESENT TENSE	PAST TENSE
я иду́	шёл (*m.*)
ты идёшь	шла (*f.*)
он идёт	шло (*n.*)
мы идём	шли́ (*pl.*)
вы идёте	
они́ иду́т	

ХОДИ́ТЬ
TO WALK (MULTIDIRECTIONAL)

PRESENT TENSE	PAST TENSE
я хожу́	regular
ты хо́дишь	
он хо́дит	
мы хо́дим	
вы хо́дите	
они́ хо́дят	

Е́ХАТЬ
TO GO BY VEHICLE (SINGLE ACTION IN ONE DIRECTION)

PRESENT TENSE	PAST TENSE
я е́ду	regular
ты е́дешь	
он е́дет	
мы е́дем	
вы е́дете	
они́ е́дут	

Essential Russian

ÉЗДИТЬ	
TO GO BY VEHICLE **(MULTIDIRECTIONAL)**	
PRESENT TENSE	**PAST TENSE**
я éзжу	regular
ты éздишь	
он éздит	
мы éздим	
вы éздите	
они́ éздят	

НЕСТИ́	
TO CARRY ON FOOT **(UNIDIRECTIONAL)**	
PRESENT TENSE	**PAST TENSE**
я несу́	нёс (*m.*)
ты несёшь	несла́ (*f.*)
он несёт	несло́ (*n.*)
мы несём	несли́ (*pl.*)
вы несёте	
они́ несу́т	

НОСИ́ТЬ	
TO CARRY ON FOOT **(MULTIDIRECTIONAL)**	
PRESENT TENSE	**PAST TENSE**
я ношу́	regular
ты но́сишь	
он но́сит	
мы но́сим	
вы но́сите	
они́ но́сят	

ВЕЗТИ́	
TO CARRY BY VEHICLE **(UNIDIRECTIONAL)**	
PRESENT TENSE	**PAST TENSE**
я везу́	вёз (*m.*)
ты везёшь	везла́ (*f.*)
он везёт	везло́ (*n.*)
мы везём	везли́ (*pl.*)
вы везёте	
они́ везу́т	

ВОЗИ́ТЬ	
TO CARRY BY VEHICLE **(MULTIDIRECTIONAL)**	
PRESENT TENSE	**PAST TENSE**
я вожу́	regular
ты во́зишь	
он во́зит	
мы во́зим	
вы во́зите	
они́ во́зят	

J. Subjunctive and conditional moods

The subjunctive and conditional in many languages constitute one of the most difficult grammatical constructions. However, in Russian they are easy and much less common. To form the subjunctive or conditional, the past tense of the verb is used together with the particle бы. Note that this form denotes the unrealizable condition only. For all real conditions, use the future tense.

если бы	*if*
е́сли бы я знал	*if I had known*
я пошёл бы	*I would have gone*
Я позвони́л бы, е́сли бы у меня́ был ваш но́мер.	*I would have called you, had I had your telephone number.*

K. Imperatives

The imperative form of a verb is derived from its third person plural present tense form. If the conjugated form has an –й– in its stem (which often "hides" in the vowels я, ю, е, or ё after vowels), use this glide and cut off the rest of the ending. If the verbal stem doesn't have an й, check the stress in the first person singular. If the stress falls on the ending, replace this ending with –и, if the stress is on the stem, with a –ь. If the ending has two consonants, always add an –и regardless of the stress pattern. For the plural imperative, simply add –те to the singular imperative form.

INFINITIVE	THIRD PERSON SINGULAR	FAMILIAR, SINGULAR	POLITE, PLURAL
писа́ть _to write_	пи́ш-ут пишу́	пиши́	пиши́те
повторя́ть _to repeat_	повторя[й-у]-т	повторя́й	повторя́йте
броса́ть _to throw_	броса[й-у]-т	броса́й	броса́йте
рабо́тать _to work_	работа[й-у]-т	рабо́тай	рабо́тайте
говори́ть _to speak_	говор-ят говорю́	говори́	говори́те
быть _to be_	бу́д-ут бу́ду	будь	бу́дьте
по́мнить _to remember_	по́мнишь	по́мни	по́мните

When forming imperatives, the reflexive verb retains its ending -ся after a consonant or -й, and -сь after a vowel.

мы́ться _to wash oneself_	мо[й-у]-тся	мо́йся	мо́йтесь

занима́ться *to study*	занима́[й-у]-тся	занима́йся	занима́йтесь
учи́ться *to study*	у́ч-атся учу́сь	учи́сь	учи́тесь

In giving an order indirectly to a third person or persons, the forms пусть and пуска́й (*coll.*) are used with the conjugated non-past form of the verb. The following verb is future perfective if the speaker assigns the task (change of state); if the speaker consents to the other party's intention, use the imperfective present verb (no change of state in the existing context).

Пусть он прочита́ет.	*Have him read (I want him to).*	Пусть он чита́ет	*Let him read (if he wants to).*
Пуска́й она́ ска́жет.	*Have her say (I want her to).*	Пусть она́ говори́т.	*Let her speak (if she wants to).*

L. Participles and gerunds

Participles and gerunds are very important parts of the Russian language, so it is necessary to know how to recognize and understand them. However, it should be made clear that they are rarely used in simple conversation, but rather in literature and more formal discourse.

Participles are verbal adjectives; gerunds are adverbials. Participles are adjectives made out of verbs. The difference between an adjective and a participle is that a participle retains the verbal qualities of tense, aspect and voice. In every other respect they are adjectives. They have three genders: masculine, feminine, and neuter. They decline the same way as adjectives and agree with the words they modify in gender, case, and number.

	PRESENT	PAST
говори́ть *to speak*	говоря́щий, –ая, –ее, –ие	говори́вший, –ая, –ее, –ие

Here's an example in the prepositional plural.

Мы говори́м о говоря́щих по-англи́йски ученика́х.

or

Мы говори́м об ученика́х, говоря́щих по-англи́йски.

We are talking about students who speak English (lit., speaking English students).

Notice that, when the entire participial phrase follows the noun it modifies, it should be surrounded by commas; no commas are needed if it precedes the noun.

Gerunds are adverbials and as such do not change, but can be imperfective and perfective. The imperfective gerunds are characterized by a simultaneous action in any tense. The perfective gerunds are used when there are two actions, one following the other; when the first action is completed, the second one starts.

IMPERFECTIVE	
чита́ть	Чита́я, он улыба́лся.
	While reading, he was smiling. (two simultaneous actions)

PERFECTIVE	
прочита́ть	Прочита́в газе́ту, он встал и ушёл.
	Having finished reading the paper, he got up and left. (one action following the other)